My First Book About Allah

Stories of Faith and Islamic Values

Aasma S.

My First Picture Book Inc

Copyright © 2024 by My First Picture Book Inc.

All rights reserved.

No portion of this book may be reproduced in any form without written permission from the publisher or author, except as permitted by U.S. copyright law.

Contents

Introduction	1
1. Allah, The Creator of the Universe	3
2. Allah's Beautiful Jannah	8
3. Allah's Endless Love	12
4. Allah's Beautiful Names	16
5. Allah's Promise in the Rainbow	22
6. Allah's Blessing in the Breeze	26
7. Allah's Nighttime Wonders	30
8. Allah, The Giver of Life	34
9. Allah's Warmth and Light	38
10. Allah's Blessing of Rain	42
11. Allah, The Most Forgiving	46

12.	Allah, The All-Knowing	50
13.	Allah's Everlasting Protection	54
14.	Allah, The Best Planner	58
15.	Allah's Beautiful Moon	62
16.	Allah's Wisdom in the Ants	66
17.	Allah's Blessing in Words: Bismillah	70
18.	Allah's Guidance through the Quran	74
19.	Allah's Wonders of the Ocean	78
20.	Allah's Beautiful Flowers	82
21.	Allah's Majesty in Mountains	86
22.	Allah, The Bountiful	90
23.	Allah's Nighttime Gift	94
24.	Allah's Gift of Life	98
25.	Allah, The Life Sustainer	102
26.	Allah's Colorful Creation	106
27.	Allah's Blessing of Friends	110

28.	Allah's Happiness in Smiles	114
29.	Allah's Gift of Ears	118
30.	Allah's Lesson in Sharing	122
31.	Allah's Help in Hard Times	126
32.	Allah's Love in Family	130
33.	Alhamdulillah: Thanking Allah	134
34.	Allah's Cycle of Night and Day	140
35.	The First Salah: Allah's Gift	144
36.	Eid: Allah's Festival of Joy	148
37.	Allah's Wisdom in Speaking Kindly	154
38.	Allah's Gift of Friendship	160
39.	Allah's Colorful Masterpiece	164
40.	Allah's Blessing in Helping Hands	168
41.	Allah's Amazing Human Body	172
42.	Allah's Colorful Butterflies	178
43.	Allah's Garden of Fairness	182

44.	Allah's Busy Bees	186
45.	Allah's Blessing of Taste	190
46.	Allah's Art in Snowflakes	194
47.	Allah's Wisdom in the Sense of Touch	198
48.	Allah's Bounty in Paradise	202
49.	Allah's Guidance in Honesty	206
50.	Allah's Knowledge in the Natural World	210

Introduction

Welcome to "My First Book About Allah," a special collection of stories created just for you! This book is filled with wonderful tales that will help you learn about Allah and His amazing creations in a fun and simple way. Each story has been written in easy-to-understand English and gentle language to make it perfect for young readers like you.

In this book, you will meet curious children who discover the beauty and wisdom in the world around them, all guided by the teachings of Allah. You will learn about the miracles of the human body, the importance of honesty, the wonders of nature, and so much more.

Our goal is to help you grow your love for Allah and appreciate His blessings in every part of life. We hope these stories inspire you to be kind, thoughtful, and grateful every day.

Enjoy reading and discovering the incredible stories in "My First Book About Allah." May Allah's blessings be with you always.

Chapter 1

Allah, The Creator of the Universe

Once upon a time, before anything else existed, there was Allah. Allah is the Creator of everything. He is very powerful and very loving. He wanted to create a beautiful world for us. So, He did.

First, Allah made the sky. The sky is like a big blue blanket over us. It is so high and so wide. During the day, the sky is blue, and at night, it is dark. But what makes the night sky so special? Stars!

Allah filled the night sky with stars. There are so many stars, more than we can count. Some stars are big, and some stars are small. They all shine brightly like little night lights. Allah made them so we would never be scared of the dark. Stars are like tiny diamonds, and they make the night sky very beautiful.

Next, Allah made the planets. Our Earth is one of these planets. It is where we live. Earth is very special because it has everything we need. It has water to drink, food to eat, and air to breathe. Allah made the Earth just right for us.

But the Earth is not alone. It has friends! These friends are other planets. Some are big, like Jupiter, and some are small, like Mercury. Each planet is different and special. They all move around the Sun, which Allah also created.

The Sun is a big, bright star. It gives us light and warmth. Without the Sun, it would be very cold and dark. Allah made the Sun to help plants grow and to keep us warm. The Sun rises in the morning and sets in the evening. This is why we have day and night.

Allah also made the Moon. The Moon is not as bright as the Sun, but it is very important. At night, the Moon lights up the sky just enough so we can see. Sometimes, the Moon looks like a big, round ball. Other times, it looks like a banana slice. The Moon changes shape because it moves around the Earth.

After making the sky, stars, planets, the Sun, and the Moon, Allah filled the Earth with wonderful things. He made the mountains, tall and strong. He made the oceans, wide and deep. He made rivers, lakes, and waterfalls. All these things are very beautiful and make our world special.

Allah also made the trees and flowers. Trees give us shade and fruit. Flowers are pretty and smell nice. Every tree and flower is different, and each one is a gift from Allah. They make the Earth colorful and lovely.

But Allah's creations did not stop there. He made animals, big and small. Lions, elephants, birds, and fish – every animal is unique. Some animals live on land, some in the water, and some can fly in the sky. Allah made each animal perfect for where it lives.

Allah also made us, people. He gave us eyes to see, ears to hear, and hearts to love. He made us special, too. We can think, talk, and play. Allah gave us families and friends to share our lives with.

Everything Allah created is wonderful. The stars, the planets, the Sun, the Moon, the Earth, the mountains, the oceans, the trees, the flowers, the animals, and us – all these things show how great Allah is. He made everything with love and care. He made everything perfect.

So, when you look at the night sky and see the stars, remember that Allah put them there just for you. When you feel the warmth of the Sun or see the beauty of a flower, remember that Allah made these things to make you happy. Allah's creations are all around us, showing us His power and love every day.

Moral of the Story: Allah created everything around us with love and care. Always remember to appreciate the beauty of the world and be thankful to Allah for His wonderful creations.

Chapter 2

Allah's Beautiful Jannah

In a peaceful village, there lived a young boy named Yusuf. Yusuf was a curious and kind-hearted boy who loved to ask questions about the world around him. He lived with his Ummi, Abu, and younger Akhi, in a cozy home filled with love and warmth.

One evening, after dinner, Yusuf sat with his Jaddi under the twinkling stars. "Jaddi, can you tell me about Jannah?" Yusuf asked, his eyes wide with curiosity.

Jaddi smiled and nodded. "Of course, Yusuf. Jannah, also known as Heaven, is a beautiful place that Allah has prepared for those who do good deeds and follow His guidance. It is a place of eternal happiness and peace."

"Jaddi, what is Jannah like?" Yusuf asked, his excitement growing.

"Jannah is more beautiful than anything we can imagine," Jaddi replied. "It is filled with gardens, rivers of milk and honey, and palaces made of gold and precious gems. There are no worries or sadness in Jannah, only joy and contentment."

Yusuf's eyes sparkled with wonder. "Are there animals in Jannah, Jaddi?"

"Yes, Yusuf," Jaddi said with a warm smile. "There are many wonderful animals in Jannah. You will see birds with colorful feathers, gentle deer, and even friendly lions. Everything in Jannah is in harmony and peace."

"How can we go to Jannah, Jaddi?" Yusuf asked, wanting to know more.

"To go to Jannah, we must follow Allah's teachings," Jaddi explained. "We should pray, be kind to others, help those in need, and always be truthful. Allah loves those who do good deeds and strive to be the best they can be."

Yusuf listened carefully. He wanted to do everything he could to please Allah. "I will try my best to do good deeds and be kind to everyone, Jaddi."

Jaddi patted Yusuf's head gently. "That's the spirit, Yusuf. Remember to always say Bismillah before you start anything and Alhamdulillah when you finish. Thanking Allah for His blessings is very important."

The next day, Yusuf woke up with a new determination. He helped his Ummi with chores, shared his toys with his Akhi, and even helped his neighbor carry groceries. Each time he did something good, he whispered, "Bismillah" before starting and "Alhamdulillah" when he finished.

As days passed, Yusuf continued to do good deeds and follow Allah's guidance. He prayed regularly, listened to his parents, and was kind to his friends. He felt a sense of peace and happiness knowing that he was on the right path.

One evening, as Yusuf lay in bed, he thought about Jannah and how beautiful it must be. He whispered a prayer, "Dear Allah, please help me be a good person and guide me to Jannah."

Moral of the Story: Jannah, or Heaven, is a beautiful place that Allah has prepared for those who do good deeds and follow His guidance. By being kind, helpful, and truthful, we can strive to enter Jannah and experience eternal happiness and peace.

Chapter 3

Allah's Endless Love

One bright and sunny morning, a little girl named Leila woke up with a big smile on her face. Today was a special day because she was going to visit her grandparents' house in the countryside.

When Leila and her parents arrived at her grandparents' house, she ran straight to the garden. Her grandma was there, watering the plants. "Assalamu Alaikum, Grandma!" Leila called out happily.

"Wa Alaikum Assalam, my dear Leila," her grandma replied with a warm smile. "Come and help me water the flowers."

Leila eagerly took the watering can and started watering the flowers. As she did, she noticed how each flower was unique and beautiful. "Grandma, who made all these lovely flowers?" Leila asked.

Her grandma gently patted her head and said, "Allah made these flowers, Leila. Allah's love is endless, and He shows His love in many beautiful ways. These flowers are one of the many gifts from Allah."

Leila's eyes widened with wonder. She looked around the garden and saw the colorful butterflies, the tall trees, and the blue sky. She felt very happy and loved. "Allah must really love us to give us so many wonderful things," she said.

"Yes, my dear," her grandma agreed. "Allah's love is everywhere. It is in the flowers, the trees, the birds, and even in the air we breathe. Allah's love is endless and surrounds us all the time."

After helping her grandma, Leila decided to explore the garden. She found a little bird with a broken wing. The bird looked scared and in pain. Leila carefully picked up the bird and brought it to her grandpa.

"Grandpa, this bird is hurt. Can we help it?" Leila asked with concern.

Her grandpa smiled and said, "Of course, Leila. Allah loves all His creatures, and we should too. Let's take care of this little bird."

They gently wrapped the bird's wing and gave it some water and seeds. Leila watched as the bird slowly began to feel better. "Thank you, Grandpa," she said. "I'm glad we could help the bird."

Her grandpa hugged her and said, "Leila, when we show kindness and love to others, we are sharing Allah's endless love. Helping the bird was a way to show our love and care, just as Allah cares for us."

That evening, as the sun was setting, Leila sat with her grandparents in the garden. They watched the sky turn orange and pink. Leila felt very peaceful and happy.

"Grandma, Grandpa," Leila said softly, "I feel so happy and loved today. I can see Allah's love everywhere."

Her grandparents smiled and nodded. "Yes, Leila," her grandma said, "Allah's love is all around us. It is endless and always with us. Remember to always be grateful for Allah's love and to share it with others."

That night, as Leila lay in bed, she whispered a prayer. "Thank you, Allah, for your endless love. Thank you for the flowers, the trees, the birds, and my family. Please help me always remember your love and share it with others."

Leila felt a warm, comforting feeling in her heart. She knew that Allah's love was always with her, no matter where she was.

Moral of the Story: Always remember to be grateful for Allah's love and to share it with everyone around you. When you help and care for others, you are sharing Allah's endless love.

Chapter 4

Allah's Beautiful Names

Once upon a time, in a peaceful village, there lived a curious little girl named Sara. Sara loved learning new things, especially about Allah. One day, her grandfather, who she called Jaddi, sat her down to tell her about Allah's beautiful names.

"Sara," Jaddi began, "did you know that Allah has many beautiful names? Each name tells us something special about Him."

Sara's eyes lit up with excitement. "Can you tell me some of them, Jaddi?" she asked.

"Of course, my dear," Jaddi said, smiling. "Let's start with **Ar-Rahman**. It means 'The Most Merciful'. Allah is very kind and merciful to all of us. He forgives us when we make mistakes and loves us very much."

Sara thought about the times she had made mistakes and how her parents always forgave her. She was happy to know that Allah was even more forgiving and loving.

"Another beautiful name of Allah is **Ar-Rahim**," Jaddi continued. "It means 'The Most Compassionate'. Allah cares for us deeply. He always wants the best for us and helps us when we are in need."

Sara remembered how her Ummi always took care of her when she was sick, making her feel better. She felt comforted knowing that Allah cared for her even more.

"Then there is **Al-Malik**," Jaddi said. "It means 'The King'. Allah is the King of everything. He is in charge of the whole world and everything in it."

Sara imagined a great king sitting on a golden throne, but she knew that Allah was even greater and more powerful than any king.

"Next, we have **Al-Quddus**," Jaddi continued. "It means 'The Pure One'. Allah is perfect and pure. He is free from any faults or mistakes."

Sara thought about how sometimes she felt sad when she did something wrong, but knowing that Allah was perfect made her feel safe and happy.

"Another important name is **As-Salam**," Jaddi said. "It means 'The Source of Peace'. Allah brings peace and happiness to our hearts. When we feel scared or worried, we can pray to Allah, and He will help us feel calm."

Sara smiled, remembering how praying to Allah always made her feel better when she was scared at night.

"One of my favorite names is **Al-Khaliq**," Jaddi said with a twinkle in his eye. "It means 'The Creator'. Allah created everything we see, like the stars, the moon, the sun, the trees, and all the animals."

Sara loved looking at the stars at night and watching the animals in the park. She felt amazed knowing that Allah had created all those wonderful things.

"Then there is **Al-Ghaffar**," Jaddi went on. "It means 'The Forgiving'. Allah forgives us when we say sorry for our mistakes. He loves us so much and always gives us another chance."

Sara thought about how good it felt to be forgiven by her parents and friends. She felt even happier knowing that Allah was always ready to forgive her too.

"Another name is **Al-Wadud**," Jaddi said. "It means 'The Loving'. Allah loves us more than anyone else. His love is endless and always with us."

Sara felt warm inside, knowing that Allah loved her so much.

"And finally, let's talk about **Al-Hakeem**," Jaddi concluded. "It means 'The Wise'. Allah is very wise and knows what is best for us. Even when we don't understand why things happen, we should trust that Allah has a good plan for us."

Sara hugged her Jaddi tightly. She felt grateful and happy to learn about Allah's beautiful names and what they mean.

Moral of the Story: Allah has many beautiful names that tell us how loving, kind, and wise He is. Remembering these names helps us feel closer to Allah and understand how much He cares for us.

Chapter 5

Allah's Promise in the Rainbow

Once upon a time, in a small village, there was a little boy named Bilal. Bilal loved to play outside, especially after it rained. One day, while he was playing, he saw something amazing in the sky. It was a big, beautiful rainbow with many colors.

Bilal ran inside to find his Ummi. "Ummi, come quick! There's a rainbow in the sky!" he shouted excitedly.

His Ummi smiled and followed him outside. They stood together and looked at the rainbow. "Do you know what the rainbow means, Bilal?" his Ummi asked.

Bilal shook his head. "No, Ummi. What does it mean?"

His Ummi sat down with him and began to explain. "A long time ago, Allah made a promise to His creations. The rainbow is a sign of that promise. It shows Allah's love and His beauty in nature."

Bilal's eyes grew wide with wonder. "Can you tell me more about Allah's promise, Ummi?"

"Of course, Bilal," his Ummi said. "Allah promised to always take care of us and the world. The rainbow is a reminder of that promise. It shows us that even after the storm, there is always something beautiful. The rainbow reminds us of Allah's love and mercy."

Bilal looked up at the rainbow again. He loved all the bright colors. "What are the colors of the rainbow, Ummi?"

His Ummi pointed to the sky and named each color. "There are seven colors in the rainbow. Red, orange, yellow, green, blue, indigo, and violet. Each color is special and shows Allah's beauty."

Bilal smiled. "I like the rainbow even more now. It's like a painting in the sky."

"Yes, Bilal," his Ummi agreed. "It's like a beautiful painting that Allah made for us. The rainbow also teaches us to be hopeful. Even when things seem difficult, Allah's promise reminds us that everything will be okay."

Bilal thought about this. He felt happy knowing that Allah cared so much about him and everyone else. "Does Allah show His promise in other ways too, Ummi?"

"Yes, Bilal," his Ummi said. "Allah's promise is also in the sunshine that makes us warm, the rain that helps plants grow, and the stars that light up the night sky. All these things show us Allah's love and care."

Bilal loved to look at the stars at night. He felt closer to Allah when he thought about how much love was in the world. "I'm glad Allah loves us so much," he said.

"Me too, Bilal," his Ummi said, giving him a hug. "Whenever you see a rainbow or the stars, remember Allah's promise and His love for us."

Bilal felt very happy and safe. He knew that Allah was always watching over him. The rainbow in the sky was like a special gift from Allah, reminding him to be hopeful and grateful.

Every time it rained, Bilal would look for the rainbow. When he saw it, he would smile and say a little prayer, thanking Allah for His promise and love. Bilal also shared the story of the rainbow with his friends, so they too could understand Allah's promise.

As the days went by, Bilal always remembered the lesson his Ummi had taught him. He knew that no matter what happened, Allah's promise was always there. The rainbow, the stars, and all of nature were signs of Allah's endless love and care.

Moral of the Story: The rainbow shows Allah's promise and His love for us. It reminds us to be hopeful and thankful for Allah's care in everything around us.

Chapter 6

Allah's Blessing in the Breeze

One sunny morning, a little girl named Aisha was playing in the park with her Jadda. They were running, laughing, and having so much fun. The sun was shining brightly, and the sky was blue. But after a while, Aisha started feeling very hot. Her face turned red, and she was sweating a lot. She didn't feel like playing anymore.

Aisha and her Jadda sat down under a big tree to rest. Suddenly, Aisha felt something soft and cool on her face. It was a gentle breeze! The breeze was like a soft touch from a loving hand. It made her feel cool and happy. Aisha closed her eyes and smiled.

Aisha looked around and saw the leaves of the trees moving. The flowers were swaying gently. The breeze made everything look like they were dancing. Aisha felt like she was dancing too. The breeze was making her feel better and more comfortable.

Aisha thought about where this wonderful breeze came from. She remembered that everything good comes from Allah. Allah loves us so much and gives us many gifts. The gentle breeze is one of those gifts. It helps us feel cool on hot days and makes us happy.

Aisha turned to her Jadda and said, "Jadda, the breeze feels so nice. It makes me feel so much better."

Her Jadda smiled and said, "Yes, my dear. Allah has given us this gentle breeze to help us feel cool and happy. Whenever you feel the breeze, remember that it is a gift from Allah."

Aisha nodded and thought about all the other gifts Allah had given her. She thought about the warm sun, the blue sky, the trees, and the flowers. She realized how much Allah loved her and how many beautiful things He had created for everyone to enjoy. Aisha felt very grateful and decided to always remember to thank Allah for all His blessings.

As Aisha and her Jadda sat under the tree, they noticed how the breeze made everything around them so much nicer. The trees, the flowers, and even the birds seemed to enjoy the cool air. The leaves rustled gently, and the flowers nodded in agreement as if they were saying thank you to the breeze. Aisha felt happy to be outside, enjoying the beautiful day that Allah had given them.

When Aisha and her Jadda went home, Aisha told her Ummi about the gentle breeze. Her Ummi smiled and said, "Yes, my dear. Allah has given us many gifts to make our lives better. The breeze is one of them. Whenever you feel the breeze, remember to thank Allah."

That night, as Aisha got ready for bed, she thought about the wonderful day she had spent at the park with her Jadda. She remembered how the gentle breeze had made her feel cool and happy. She knelt down and prayed to Allah. "Thank you, Allah, for the gentle breeze and all the other beautiful gifts you have given us," she said. "Thank you for loving us and taking care of us."

Aisha felt very happy and peaceful as she finished her prayer. She climbed into bed and closed her eyes, thinking about all the wonderful things Allah had given her. As she drifted off to sleep, she felt a gentle breeze coming through the open window. It was as if Allah was reminding her of His love and care.

The next day, Aisha woke up with a big smile on her face. She was excited to go back to the park and enjoy another beautiful day. She knew that whenever she felt the gentle breeze, it was a special touch from Allah, who loved her very much.

Moral of the Story: Allah loves us very much and gives us many wonderful gifts. The gentle breeze is one of those gifts. It cools us down and makes us feel happy. Always remember to thank Allah for His blessings. When you feel the breeze, think of it as a special touch from Allah, who loves you very much.

Chapter 7

Allah's Nighttime Wonders

Once upon a time, in a small village, there was a little boy named Ali. Ali loved to play outside during the day, but his favorite time was at night. He loved looking up at the night sky to see the bright, twinkling stars.

One evening, after dinner, Ali asked his Abu, "Can we go outside to look at the stars?"

His Abu smiled and said, "Of course, Ali. Let's go."

They went outside and lay on a soft blanket in the garden. The sky was dark, and the stars were shining brightly. Ali's eyes sparkled with excitement. "Why are the stars so bright, Abu?" he asked.

His Abu began to explain. "The stars are a special creation of Allah. Allah made the stars to light up the night sky. They remind us of His greatness and His power."

Ali listened carefully. "What do the stars do, Abu?"

"The stars do many things, Ali," his Abu said. "They help sailors find their way at sea, and they help travelers find their way at night. Long ago, people used the stars to make maps and to know the seasons. The stars are like tiny lamps in the sky, showing us the beauty of Allah's creation."

Ali thought about this and felt amazed. "Can you tell me more about the night sky, Abu?"

"Sure, Ali," his Abu replied. "The night sky is full of wonders. Sometimes, you can see the moon, which changes its shape every night. There are also planets, which look like bright stars but are different. Allah made all these things to show us His beautiful creation."

Ali loved looking at the moon, too. "Why does the moon change its shape, Abu?"

"The moon changes its shape because of how it moves around the Earth," his Abu explained. "Sometimes we see the whole moon, and sometimes we only see a part of it. This is another amazing thing that Allah created for us to see and enjoy."

Ali felt very happy. He loved learning about the stars and the moon. "What else can we see in the night sky, Abu?"

His Abu smiled. "Sometimes, if we are lucky, we can see shooting stars. These are tiny bits of rock that burn up when they come close to Earth. They look like bright streaks of light in the sky. And sometimes, we can see the Milky Way, which is a big group of stars that looks like a white path across the sky. All these things show us how amazing Allah's creation is."

Ali looked up at the sky with wonder. "I want to see a shooting star one day," he said.

His Abu nodded. "It's a beautiful sight, Ali. The night sky is full of surprises. Always remember that Allah made the stars and everything in the sky for us to marvel at and enjoy."

From that day on, Ali always enjoyed his time under the night sky. Ali felt very grateful. He thanked Allah for making such a beautiful night sky. He loved the stars, the moon, and all the wonders he could see. He knew that Allah had made the night sky just for us to marvel at and enjoy.

Moral of the Story: The night sky and the stars are a beautiful creation of Allah. They remind us of His greatness and His love for us. Always remember to look up and enjoy the wonders of the night sky.

Chapter 8

Allah, The Giver of Life

Once upon a time, in a small village, there was a little girl named Fatima. Fatima loved spending time with her family and playing with her friends. One day, she asked her Ummi, "Ummi, who gives us the food we eat and the water we drink?"

Her Ummi smiled and said, "Allah is the Provider. He gives us everything we need."

Fatima was curious. "How does Allah provide for us, Ummi?"

Her Ummi sat down with her and began to explain. "Allah gives us food in many ways. He makes the sun shine and the rain fall so plants can grow. These plants give us fruits, vegetables, and grains."

Fatima listened carefully. "What about the bread we eat? How does Allah provide that?"

"Bread comes from wheat," her Ummi explained. "Farmers plant the seeds, and with Allah's help, the wheat grows tall. Then, they harvest the wheat, grind it into flour, and bake it into bread. Allah helps the farmers and gives us the wheat to make bread."

Fatima thought about this. She loved eating fresh bread with her meals. "And what about water, Ummi? How does Allah give us water?"

"Allah gives us water through rain," her Ummi said. "The rain fills the rivers, lakes, and streams. It also goes into the ground, where we can get it from wells. Water helps plants grow and keeps us alive. It is a precious gift from Allah."

Fatima felt grateful for the rain and the water they had. "What else does Allah provide for us, Ummi?"

Her Ummi continued, "Allah provides us with animals, too. Cows give us milk, chickens give us eggs, and fish from the rivers and seas are food for us. Allah also gives us the air we breathe and the sunshine that warms us."

Fatima loved drinking milk and eating eggs for breakfast. She realized how much Allah cared for them. "How does Allah help the animals, Ummi?"

"Allah helps the animals by giving them food and water, too," her Ummi replied. "He makes the grass grow for cows and sheep to eat. He provides insects and plants for birds and other animals. Allah takes care of all His creations."

Fatima was amazed at how Allah provided for everyone. "I didn't know Allah did so much for us and the animals," she said.

Her Ummi smiled. "Yes, Fatima. Allah's love and care are everywhere. He gives us everything we need to live and be happy."

Fatima hugged her Ummi. "Shukran, Ummi, for telling me about Allah, the Provider. I will always remember to be thankful for everything we have."

From that day on, every time she ate a meal or drank water, Fatima remembered that it was a gift from Allah. She also shared this special lesson with her friends, so they too could understand how Allah provides for everyone.

As the days passed, Fatima always appreciated the blessings Allah had given them. She knew that no matter what, Allah would always provide for them and take care of them.

Moral of the Story: Allah is the Provider who gives us food, water, and everything we need. Always remember to be thankful for Allah's blessings.

Chapter 9

Allah's Warmth and Light

Once upon a time, in a small village, there was a little boy named Hassan. Hassan loved to play outside with his friends. He enjoyed running in the fields, playing with his toys, and looking at the beautiful sky. One day, while he was playing, he noticed how warm and bright the day was.

Hassan ran inside to find his Ummi. "Ummi, why is it so bright and warm outside?" he asked.

His Ummi smiled and said, "Hassan, it is because of the sun. The sun is a blessing from Allah. It gives us light and warmth every day."

Hassan was curious. "How does the sun give us light and warmth, Ummi?"

His Ummi sat down with him and began to explain. "The sun is like a big, glowing ball in the sky. It shines its light on the Earth, making everything bright. The sun's light helps us see during the day. Without the sun, it would be very dark."

Hassan listened carefully. He liked playing outside when it was bright. "And how does the sun keep us warm?"

"The sun's rays give us warmth," his Ummi explained. "When the sun shines, it makes the air, the ground, and the water warm. This warmth helps plants grow and keeps us comfortable. Without the sun, it would be very cold, and plants would not grow well."

Hassan thought about this. He loved the bright and warm days when he could play outside. "What else does the sun do, Ummi?"

"The sun does many wonderful things, Hassan," his Ummi continued. "It helps plants make their food through a process called photosynthesis. Plants use the sun's light to grow strong and healthy. These plants give us fruits, vegetables, and grains to eat."

Hassan looked at the garden outside and saw the plants and trees. "So, the sun helps our garden grow?"

"Yes, Hassan," his Ummi said. "The sun helps our garden grow. It also helps farmers grow crops in their fields. The food we eat, like rice, wheat, and corn, all grow because of the sun's light and warmth."

Hassan felt grateful for the sun. "Does the sun help animals too, Ummi?"

"Of course, Hassan," his Ummi replied. "The sun helps animals by keeping them warm and helping plants grow, which many animals eat. It also helps birds and other animals find their way because they can see clearly during the day."

Hassan thought about the birds and animals he saw every day. "I didn't know the sun did so many things. It's amazing!"

His Ummi nodded. "Yes, Hassan. Allah made the sun to help all His creations. The sun gives us light, warmth, and helps plants and animals. It is a very special blessing from Allah."

Hassan hugged his Ummi. "Shukran, Ummi, for telling me about the sun. I will always be thankful for its light and warmth."

From that day on, Hassan always noticed the sun. He loved how it made the day bright and warm. Whenever he felt the sun's warmth on his face, he remembered that it was a blessing from Allah. Hassan also shared what he had learned with his friends, so they too could understand how special the sun was.

Moral of the Story: The sun is a blessing from Allah. It gives us light and warmth, helps plants grow, and provides for all of Allah's creations. Always remember to be thankful for the sun and its many blessings.

Chapter 10

Allah's Blessing of Rain

Once upon a time, in a small village, there was a little girl named Leila. Leila loved the rain. She loved how it made everything fresh and green. One day, while she was watching the rain from her window, she asked her Jadda, "Jadda, why is the rain so important?"

Her Jadda smiled and said, "Leila, the rain is very special. Just as the rain nurtures the earth, Allah's mercy nurtures our hearts."

Leila was curious. "How does the rain nurture the earth, Jadda?"

Her Jadda began to explain. "The rain gives water to the plants, flowers, and trees. It helps them grow strong and healthy. Without rain, the plants would not be able to grow, and the earth would be dry and barren."

Leila thought about the beautiful garden outside. She loved the colorful flowers and the tall trees. "So, the rain helps our garden grow?"

"Yes, Leila," her Jadda said. "The rain helps our garden grow. It also fills the rivers, lakes, and streams. Animals drink the water from these places to stay healthy. Rain is a blessing from Allah."

Leila listened carefully. "How is Allah's mercy like the rain, Jadda?"

"Allah's mercy is like the rain because it helps us grow and feel happy," her Jadda explained. "Just as the rain nurtures the earth, Allah's mercy nurtures our hearts. It makes us feel loved and cared for."

Leila felt happy hearing this. "Can you tell me more about Allah's mercy, Jadda?"

"Of course, Leila," her Jadda replied. "Allah's mercy is in many things. It is in the love we feel from our family and friends. It is in the help we get when we are in trouble. Allah's mercy is always with us, just like the rain."

Leila thought about the times when she felt sad or scared, and how her family and friends helped her feel better. "So, Allah's mercy is always with us, Jadda?"

"Yes, Leila," her Jadda said. "Allah's mercy is always with us. When we are kind to others, when we share, and when we help someone in need, we are showing Allah's mercy."

Leila smiled. She wanted to show Allah's mercy too. "What can I do to show Allah's mercy, Jadda?"

"You can be kind to others, Leila," her Jadda said. "You can share your toys, help your friends, and be polite. When you do these things, you are showing Allah's mercy to others."

Leila felt excited. She wanted to be kind and helpful. "I will try my best, Jadda."

Her Jadda hugged her and said, "That's wonderful, Leila. Remember, just as the rain helps the earth grow, your kindness will help others feel happy and loved."

From that day on, Leila always remembered the lesson her Jadda taught her. She loved the rain even more because it reminded her of Allah's mercy. She tried to be kind and helpful every day, showing Allah's mercy to everyone around her.

Moral of the Story: Allah's mercy is like the rain. Just as the rain helps the earth grow, Allah's mercy helps our hearts feel loved and happy. Always remember to be kind and show Allah's mercy to others.

Chapter 11

Allah, The Most Forgiving

Once upon a time, in a small village, there was a little boy named Omar. Omar loved playing with his friends and having fun. One day, while playing, Omar accidentally broke his friend Ali's favorite toy. Ali felt very sad and upset.

Omar felt bad for what he had done. He went home and told his Ummi about it. "Ummi, I broke Ali's toy, and now he is very sad. What should I do?" Omar asked.

His Ummi sat down with him and said, "Omar, when we make a mistake, it is important to say sorry. Allah is the Most Forgiving, and He loves it when we ask for forgiveness and try to make things right."

Omar listened carefully. "How do I say sorry, Ummi?"

"First, you need to tell Ali that you are sorry for breaking his toy," his Ummi explained. "Then, you can ask Allah to forgive you for your mistake."

Omar nodded. He wanted to make things right with Ali and ask for Allah's forgiveness. "How do I ask Allah to forgive me, Ummi?"

"You can make a dua," his Ummi said. "Say, 'Oh Allah, I am sorry for my mistake. Please forgive me and help me to be better.' Allah is very kind and loves to forgive us when we say sorry and mean it."

The next day, Omar went to find Ali. He felt a little nervous but remembered what his Ummi had said. "Ali, I am very sorry for breaking your toy. It was an accident, and I didn't mean to hurt you," Omar said.

Ali looked at Omar and saw that he was truly sorry. "It's okay, Omar. I forgive you," Ali said with a smile.

Omar felt very happy. He had said sorry to Ali, and Ali had forgiven him. Omar also remembered to ask Allah for forgiveness. He made a dua, saying, "Oh Allah, I am sorry for my mistake. Please forgive me and help me to be better."

Omar's Ummi saw how happy he was and said, "See, Omar, Allah is the Most Forgiving. When we say sorry and ask for forgiveness, Allah forgives us and helps us to be better."

Omar felt very grateful. He wanted to be a good friend and always ask for forgiveness when he made a mistake. "Shukran, Ummi, for teaching me about Allah's forgiveness."

From that day on, Omar always remembered the lesson his Ummi had taught him. Whenever he made a mistake, he would say sorry and ask for forgiveness. He felt happy knowing that Allah was always there to forgive him and help him be better.

Omar also shared this lesson with his friends. He told them, "When we make a mistake, it's important to say sorry and ask for forgiveness. Allah is the Most Forgiving and loves it when we try to make things right."

His friends listened and agreed. They all promised to be kind and say sorry when they made mistakes. They knew that Allah's forgiveness was a beautiful gift that helped them be better friends and better people.

Moral of the Story: Allah is the Most Forgiving. When we make a mistake, it is important to say sorry and ask for forgiveness. Always remember to be kind and make things right.

Chapter 12

Allah, The All-Knowing

One beautiful morning, a little boy named Omar woke up feeling curious. Today, he was going to visit his Jaddi's farm.

When Omar arrived at the farm, his Jaddi greeted him with a big smile. "Assalamu Alaikum, Omar! Are you ready to explore the farm today?"

"Wa Alaikum Assalam, Jaddi! Yes, I am ready!" Omar replied excitedly.

Jaddi took him to see the animals first. There were cows, sheep, chickens, and even a horse. Omar noticed that each animal had its own way of living. The cows were chewing grass, the chickens were pecking at seeds, and the sheep were resting under a tree.

"Jaddi, how do the animals know what to eat and where to go?" Omar asked.

Jaddi smiled and said, "Allah, The All-Knowing, has given each animal the knowledge they need to survive. Allah knows everything, and He guides all His creations."

Omar was amazed. He thought about how Allah must know everything about everyone and everything. It made him feel very special to be cared for by Allah, who knows so much.

Next, Jaddi showed him the vegetable garden. There were rows of tomatoes, cucumbers, and carrots. Omar pointed to a tiny seedling and asked, "How does this little plant know how to grow into a big tomato plant?"

"That is because Allah, The All-Knowing, has created each plant with the ability to grow and produce food," Jaddi explained. "Allah knows what every plant needs – sunlight, water, and good soil. He has made sure they have everything to grow strong."

Omar nodded, thinking about how wonderful it was that Allah knew exactly what each plant needed. He helped Jaddi water the plants and enjoyed seeing how healthy and green they were.

Afterwards, they both sat under a big tree to rest. Omar looked up at the sky and saw birds flying. He wondered how the birds knew where to fly and how to build their nests. "Jaddi, how do the birds know what to do?"

Jaddi replied, "Allah, The All-Knowing, has given the birds the knowledge to fly, find food, and build nests. Allah's knowledge is perfect, and He has provided everything in nature with the guidance it needs."

Omar felt very grateful to learn about how Allah's knowledge helps all living things. He realized that Allah's wisdom is everywhere, from the smallest seed to the largest animal.

As the sun began to set, Jaddi said, "Let's thank Allah for all the wonderful things He has created and for His endless knowledge that guides us."

Omar joined Jaddi in a short prayer. "Thank you, Allah, for your perfect knowledge and for guiding all your creations. Help us always remember your wisdom and care."

That night, as Omar lay in bed, he thought about everything he had learned at the farm. He felt safe and loved knowing that Allah, The All-Knowing, was always watching over him and guiding him. He whispered a prayer, "Thank you, Allah, for knowing everything and for taking care of us all."

Moral of the Story: Always remember that Allah, The All-Knowing, is watching over you and caring for you. Trust in His wisdom and be grateful for His endless knowledge.

Chapter 13

Allah's Everlasting Protection

One bright and sunny day, a little girl named Maryam was excited to go on a picnic with her family. They packed a basket with delicious food, a blanket, and some toys. They all loved spending time together outdoors.

When they arrived at the park, they found a nice spot under a big, shady tree. Maryam ran around happily, playing with her ball.

After a while, Maryam saw a beautiful butterfly fluttering near the flowers. She wanted to catch it and show it to her parents. She followed the butterfly as it flew from flower to flower. But soon, she realized that she had wandered far away from her parents.

Maryam looked around and couldn't see her family. She felt scared and alone. The park suddenly seemed big and unfamiliar. She started to cry, calling out for her parents.

Meanwhile, Maryam's Ummi noticed that she was not nearby. She quickly got up and began looking for her. Her Abu followed, feeling worried. They called out Maryam's name, searching for her.

Maryam remembered what her parents always told her. "Allah is always with us," they said. "When you are scared or lost, pray to Allah for help."

Through her tears, Maryam whispered a prayer, "Oh Allah, please help me find my parents. Please protect me."

Just then, Maryam heard her Ummi's voice calling her name. She followed the sound and soon saw her parents running towards her. Maryam ran to them, feeling relieved and safe. Her Ummi hugged her tightly, and her Abu patted her back.

"We were so worried about you, Maryam," her Ummi said. "Are you okay?"

Maryam nodded, still holding onto her Ummi. "I got scared when I couldn't find you," she said. "But I remembered to pray to Allah, and then I heard your voice."

Her Ummi smiled and kissed Maryam's forehead. "Allah is always protecting us," she said. "He helped us find you quickly. Always remember that Allah is with you, no matter where you are."

Her Abu added, "We are never alone, Maryam. Allah's protection is with us everywhere. When you feel scared or lost, just pray to Allah, and He will guide you."

They all walked back to their picnic spot, feeling grateful for Allah's protection. Maryam's parents reminded her to stay close and always be careful. They enjoyed the rest of their picnic together, playing games and sharing stories.

As the sun began to set, they packed up their things and headed home. Maryam felt happy and peaceful, knowing that Allah was always looking out for her. That night, before going to bed, Maryam said her prayers.

"Thank you, Allah, for protecting me and helping me find my parents today," Maryam prayed. "Please keep watching over us and keeping us safe."

Maryam's parents also thanked Allah for His protection. They were grateful for the blessings of the day and for their family's safety.

Moral of the Story: Allah's protection is always with us. He watches over us and keeps us safe, even when we feel scared or lost. Always remember to pray to Allah and trust in His protection. Allah loves us and is always there to protect us.

Chapter 14

Allah, The Best Planner

Once upon a time, in a small village, there lived a boy named Hamza. Hamza was very excited because his family planned to go on a picnic in the mountains. He had been looking forward to this day for a long time.

The night before the picnic, Hamza packed his favorite toys, a soccer ball, and some snacks. He went to bed early, dreaming of all the fun he would have the next day.

When Hamza woke up, he saw dark clouds in the sky. "Oh no," he thought, "I hope it doesn't rain." He quickly got dressed and ran to the kitchen where his parents were having breakfast.

"Good morning, Ummi and Abu," Hamza said. "Do you think we can still go on the picnic?"

His Abu looked out the window and said, "It looks like it might rain, Hamza. But let's wait a little and see."

Hamza felt worried. He really wanted to go on the picnic. He prayed, "Dear Allah, please don't let it rain so we can go to the mountains."

After breakfast, the rain started to pour. Hamza felt very sad. His Ummi hugged him and said, "Hamza, sometimes things don't go as we plan. But remember, Allah is the best planner. He knows what's best for us."

Hamza tried to understand, but he still felt disappointed. His Abu said, "Let's do something fun at home today. We can have an indoor picnic!"

They spread a big blanket in the living room and put all the food and snacks on it. Hamza's Ummi made sandwiches and his Abu brought juice and fruit. They played games, told stories, and had a wonderful time together.

While they were having their indoor picnic, Hamza's friend, Amina, came over. She had an umbrella and was all wet from the rain. "Can I join you?" she asked.

"Of course!" Hamza said, happy to see his friend. Amina joined them on the blanket, and they played more games and laughed a lot.

As the day went on, the rain kept falling. Hamza noticed how much fun they were having indoors. He realized that even though they didn't go to the mountains, the day turned out to be special in a different way.

In the evening, the rain stopped. The sun came out, and there was a beautiful rainbow in the sky. Hamza, Amina, and his parents went outside to see the rainbow. It was so colorful and bright.

Hamza's Abu said, "See, Hamza, even though it rained and we couldn't go on our picnic, we still had a wonderful day. Allah had a different plan for us, and it turned out great."

Hamza smiled and felt grateful. He learned that sometimes, even when things don't go as planned, Allah's plan is always the best.

That night, as Hamza got ready for bed, he thanked Allah for the fun day he had. He remembered to always trust in Allah's plans, knowing that Allah always knows what is best.

Hamza fell asleep with a happy heart, dreaming of more adventures and trusting in Allah's perfect plans.

Moral of the Story: Trust in Allah's plans, even when things don't go as we expect. Allah always knows what is best for us.

Chapter 15

Allah's Beautiful Moon

Once upon a time, in a small village, there was a little girl named Zara. Zara loved to look at the night sky. She thought the stars were like tiny diamonds, and the moon was the most beautiful of all.

One night, Zara noticed that the moon looked different. It was a thin crescent, like a smile in the sky. Curious, Zara asked her Abu, "Abu, why does the moon look different tonight?"

Her Abu smiled and said, "Zara, the moon changes its shape every night. This is called the phases of the moon. Let me tell you a story about it."

Zara sat beside her Abu, ready to listen.

"Allah created the moon, and it has a special job. The moon lights up the night sky and helps us keep track of time. The moon doesn't have its own light. It reflects the light of the sun."

Zara was amazed. "Wow, Abu! The moon is so special. Can you tell me more about the phases?"

"Of course," her Abu said. "There are several phases of the moon. Let's start with the new moon. During the new moon, the moon is between the Earth and the sun. We can't see it because the side that is lit by the sun is facing away from us."

Zara imagined the new moon, hidden in the sky. "What comes next, Abu?"

"After the new moon, we see a waxing crescent," her Abu continued. "This is when a small part of the moon is visible, like the smile you saw tonight. It grows bigger every night until it becomes a first quarter moon, which looks like a half-circle."

Zara nodded, picturing the crescent moon getting bigger. "And then?"

"Next is the waxing gibbous," her Abu said. "The moon is more than half visible but not yet full. After that, we have the full moon. The entire face of the moon is lit up, and it shines brightly in the sky."

Zara's eyes sparkled with excitement. "I love the full moon! It's so bright and beautiful."

"Yes, it is," her Abu agreed. "After the full moon, the moon starts to get smaller. This is called waning. First, we see the waning gibbous, then the last quarter, which is another half-moon. Finally, we have the waning crescent, a small sliver of the moon, before it becomes a new moon again."

Zara thought about the different phases. "So, the moon changes shape every night?"

"Yes," her Abu said. "It takes about 29 days for the moon to go through all its phases. Allah made the moon's cycle perfect, and it helps us know the passage of time."

Zara felt grateful for the moon and its phases. "Shukran, Abu. I love learning about Allah's creations."

That night, Zara and her Abu went outside to look at the moon again. The crescent moon smiled down at them, and Zara felt happy knowing how special the moon was.

Her Abu said, "Zara, always remember that Allah's creations are beautiful and have a purpose. The moon is a wonderful example of Allah's wisdom and care."

Zara nodded, feeling proud and thankful. She knew that every time she looked at the moon, she would remember its special phases and the beauty of Allah's creation.

Moral of the Story: Allah's creations are beautiful and have a special purpose. Always be thankful and appreciate the wonders around us.

Chapter 16

Allah's Wisdom in the Ants

One sunny morning, a little girl named Amina was playing in her backyard with her younger brother, Bilal. They loved exploring nature and discovering new things together. As they were looking around, Amina saw a tiny ant carrying a crumb much bigger than itself. She called out to Bilal excitedly.

"Bilal, come look at this tiny ant! It's carrying a huge crumb!" Amina said.

Bilal ran over and watched in amazement. "Wow, how can such a small ant carry something so big?" he asked.

Their mother, who was sitting nearby, noticed their curiosity. "Assalamu Alaikum, Amina and Bilal," she said. "What are you both looking at?"

"Wa Alaikum Assalam, Mama," they replied. "We're watching this tiny ant. It's so small, but it's carrying such a big crumb! How can it do that?"

Their mother smiled and said, "Ants are very strong and hardworking. Allah has given them the ability to carry things much bigger than themselves. Would you like to follow the ant and see where it goes?"

Amina and Bilal nodded eagerly. They carefully followed the ant as it moved across the grass, up a small hill, and through the garden. The ant never stopped, even though the crumb was very heavy. It kept going, step by step.

They noticed other ants along the way, all working hard and carrying food back to their nest. Amina and Bilal saw how the ants helped each other, making sure everyone had enough to eat. They were impressed by the ants' teamwork and determination.

"Look, Mama!" Bilal called out. "The ants are all helping each other. They never give up!"

Their mother nodded. "Yes, Bilal. Allah has taught the ants to work together and be strong. They remind us that with hard work and faith in Allah, we can achieve great things."

As they watched, the tiny ant finally reached its nest. It placed the crumb down, and other ants came to help break it into smaller pieces. They all worked together to store the food for later. The tiny ant looked very happy and proud.

Amina and Bilal felt a warm feeling in their hearts. They realized that even though they were small, they could do great things too, just like the tiny ant. Amina looked up at her mother and said, "Mama, I want to be like the ant. I want to work hard and help others."

Bilal nodded in agreement. "Me too, Mama. I want to be strong and helpful."

Their mother smiled and hugged them both. "That's a wonderful idea, Amina and Bilal. Remember, Allah is always with us, and He helps those who work hard and do good deeds. Just like the tiny ant, you can achieve anything with patience and faith."

That evening, Amina and Bilal helped their mother with the chores. They washed the dishes, cleaned their rooms, and even helped set the table for dinner. They felt proud of themselves for working hard and being helpful.

Before going to bed, Amina and Bilal whispered a prayer together, "Thank you, Allah, for teaching us about the tiny ant. Please help us to always work hard and be helpful, just like the ant."

They felt a sense of peace and happiness as they drifted off to sleep. They knew that Allah was always with them, guiding them and helping them to be strong and kind.

Moral of the Story: The tiny ant shows us that with hard work, teamwork, and faith in Allah, we can achieve great things. Always remember to work hard, help others, and trust in Allah's guidance.

Chapter 17

Allah's Blessing in Words: Bismillah

One beautiful morning, a little boy named Yusuf was getting ready for his first day of school. He was very excited but also a little nervous. His Ummi was helping him pack his backpack with all the things he would need for the day.

He took a deep breath and tried to calm his nerves. Then he remembered something his Ummi always told him. "Ummi, should I say Bismillah before I go to school?"

His Ummi smiled and nodded. "Yes, my dear. Saying Bismillah before you start anything is very important. It means 'In the name of Allah,' and it reminds us that Allah is with us and helps us."

Yusuf felt a little better knowing that Allah would be with him. He whispered, "Bismillah," and they headed out the door.

On the way to school, Yusuf saw his friend, Hasan, walking with his Abu. "Assalamu Alaikum, Hasan!" Yusuf called out.

"Wa Alaikum Assalam, Yusuf!" Hasan replied. "Are you ready for your first day of school?"

Yusuf nodded and said, "Yes, I am. I said Bismillah before I left home, so I know Allah is with me."

Hasan's Abu smiled and said, "That's wonderful, Yusuf. Saying Bismillah brings blessings and protection from Allah."

When they arrived at school, Yusuf and Hasan found their classroom and met their teacher, Mrs. Amina. She welcomed all the students with a warm smile.

"Good morning, everyone," Mrs. Amina said. "Before we start our day, let's all say Bismillah together."

The children all said, "Bismillah," and began their lessons. Yusuf felt calm and ready to learn, knowing that Allah was with him.

During lunch, Yusuf sat with Hasan and a few other friends. They opened their lunch boxes and remembered to say Bismillah before eating. "Bismillah," they all said together. The food tasted even better knowing they had asked for Allah's blessings.

After lunch, the children went outside to play. Yusuf saw a boy named Ali sitting alone. He looked sad, so Yusuf went over to him. "Assalamu Alaikum, Ali. Do you want to play with us?" he asked.

Ali looked up and smiled. "Wa Alaikum Assalam, Yusuf. I was feeling a little lonely. Thank you for inviting me."

"Let's say Bismillah and play together," Yusuf suggested.

They said, "Bismillah," and started playing. Soon, they were all laughing and having a great time.

When it was time to go home, Yusuf felt happy about his first day of school. He had made new friends and learned many new things.

At home, Yusuf told his Ummi all about his day. "Ummi, saying Bismillah made everything better. I wasn't scared, my lunch tasted good, and I made a new friend," Yusuf said.

His Ummi hugged him and said, "I'm so proud of you, Yusuf. Always remember to say Bismillah before you start anything. It brings blessings and reminds us that Allah is always with us."

That night, before going to bed, Yusuf whispered a prayer, "Thank you, Allah, for a wonderful day. Please help me to always remember to say Bismillah."

Moral of the Story: Saying Bismillah before you start anything is very important. It means "In the name of Allah" and reminds us that Allah is always with us. It brings blessings and protection. Always remember to say Bismillah and trust in Allah's guidance.

Chapter 18

Allah's Guidance through the Quran

One sunny afternoon, a little girl named Maryam was playing in her backyard. She loved to explore and find new things. On this particular day, she was pretending to be an explorer, searching for hidden treasures.

As she was playing, her Baba called her inside. "Maryam, it's time for our daily Quran reading," he said. Maryam was excited because she loved listening to stories from the Quran.

She washed her hands and sat down with her Baba. Her Baba opened the Quran and began to read. "Today, we will read a verse about Allah's guidance," he said. He recited a verse and then explained its meaning in simple words.

"Allah has sent us the Quran to guide us," he said. "It helps us know what is right and wrong. It teaches us how to be kind, honest, and good to others."

Maryam listened carefully. "Baba, how does the Quran guide us?" she asked.

Her Baba smiled. "The Quran is like a light that shows us the right path. When we read it and follow its teachings, we can make good choices and live happily."

Maryam nodded. "Just like when I follow a map on my treasure hunt," she said.

"Exactly," her Baba replied. "Allah's words in the Quran help us find the best way to live our lives."

After their reading, Maryam went back outside to play. As she continued her pretend treasure hunt, she thought about what her Baba had said. She wanted to try and follow the guidance of the Quran in her daily life.

Later that day, Maryam saw her friend, Aisha, looking sad. Aisha had lost her favorite toy and couldn't find it anywhere. Maryam remembered a lesson from the Quran about helping others. She decided to help Aisha.

"Aisha, don't worry. I will help you find your toy," Maryam said. They searched together and soon found the toy under a bush. Aisha was very happy and thanked Maryam.

"You're welcome, Aisha," Maryam said. "I remembered that the Quran teaches us to help our friends."

Aisha smiled. "That's really nice, Maryam. I want to learn more about the Quran too."

Maryam felt proud that she had followed the guidance of the Quran. When she got home, she told her Baba about what happened.

Her Baba hugged her. "I'm very proud of you, Maryam. Following the Quran's guidance makes Allah happy and helps us be good people."

That evening, before going to bed, Maryam sat with her Baba. He told her more about the importance of the Quran.

"The Quran is a gift from Allah," her Baba said. "It is full of wisdom and guidance. If you read it and follow its teachings, it will help you in every part of your life."

Maryam listened carefully. She understood how important the Quran was and decided to read it every day to learn more.

As Maryam lay in bed, she whispered a prayer, "Thank you, Allah, for the Quran. Please help me to always follow your guidance and be a good person."

Moral of the Story: The Quran is a special book from Allah that guides us in our daily lives. It teaches us to be kind, honest, and helpful. Always remember to read the Quran and follow its teachings, and it will help you make good choices and live happily.

Chapter 19

Allah's Wonders of the Ocean

Once upon a time, in a small village, there lived a curious little girl named Layla. Layla loved learning about the world around her. One day, her Ummi told her they were going to visit the beach. Layla was very excited because she had never seen the ocean before.

When they arrived at the beach, Layla saw the big, blue ocean for the first time. She ran to the edge of the water and watched the waves splash against the shore. "Ummi, the ocean is so beautiful!" she exclaimed.

Her Ummi smiled and said, "Yes, Layla. The ocean is one of Allah's wonderful creations. There are many amazing creatures and beautiful things in the ocean. Let me tell you about some of them."

Layla sat down on the sand, eager to listen to her Ummi's stories.

"First," her Ummi began, "let me tell you about dolphins. Dolphins are very smart animals. They can jump high out of the water and do flips. They live in groups called pods and help each other. Allah made dolphins very special."

Layla imagined dolphins jumping and playing in the water. "Wow, Ummi! Dolphins sound amazing. What else lives in the ocean?"

Her Ummi continued, "There are also colorful fish. Some fish are small and bright like the clownfish, which is orange with white stripes. Others are big and strong like the tuna. Allah made each fish unique and beautiful."

Layla thought about all the different fish swimming in the ocean. She was excited to learn more.

"Do you know about sea turtles?" her Ummi asked. "Sea turtles are gentle creatures. They swim long distances in the ocean. When it's time to lay eggs, they come to the beach. Baby sea turtles hatch from the eggs and crawl to the sea. Allah gave sea turtles a strong sense of direction."

Layla smiled, thinking about the baby turtles making their way to the ocean. "I love sea turtles, Ummi. What other creatures are there?"

"There are also octopuses," her Ummi said. "Octopuses have eight arms and can change color to hide from danger. They are very clever and can solve puzzles. Allah made octopuses very smart."

Layla was amazed. "Octopuses can change color? That's incredible!"

"Yes," her Ummi replied. "And there are even more wonders. There are starfish with five arms, jellyfish that glow in the dark, and crabs that walk sideways. Each creature is special in its own way."

Layla looked out at the ocean, feeling grateful for all the amazing creatures Allah had created. "Ummi, can we see some of these creatures today?"

Her Ummi nodded. "We can look for some crabs and small fish in the shallow water. But remember, Layla, always be gentle and careful with Allah's creatures."

Layla and her Ummi walked along the beach, looking for crabs and fish. Layla watched them with wonder and joy.

"Ummi, thank you for telling me about the ocean's wonders," Layla said. "Allah's creations are so amazing."

Her Ummi hugged her and said, "Yes, Layla. Allah's creations are truly wonderful. Always remember to appreciate and take care of them."

Moral of the Story: Allah's creations in the ocean are amazing and beautiful. We should appreciate and take care of them.

Chapter 20

Allah's Beautiful Flowers

One sunny morning, a little girl named Leila woke up with a big smile on her face. Today was a special day because her Jadda had promised to take her to the flower garden.

After breakfast, Leila and her Jadda set off for the garden. When they arrived, Leila was amazed by the sight before her. There were flowers of every color and shape imaginable.

"Subhan Allah, look at all these beautiful flowers, Jadda," Leila exclaimed.

"Yes, Leila," her Jadda replied. "Allah has created such wonderful things for us to enjoy. Each flower is unique and shows us the beauty of Allah's creation."

Leila and her Jadda walked through the garden, admiring the flowers. Leila bent down to smell a red rose. "It smells so nice, Jadda. How did Allah make flowers smell so good?"

Her Jadda smiled and said, "Allah is Al-Khaliq, the Creator. He made everything in the world with love and care. Flowers have beautiful colors and sweet smells to make the world more beautiful and to remind us of His greatness."

As they continued walking, they saw a gardener working in the garden. The gardener was planting new flowers and taking care of the old ones. Leila watched him curiously.

"Jadda, what is the gardener doing?" she asked.

"The gardener is planting new flowers and taking care of the ones that are already here," her Jadda explained. "Just like Allah takes care of us, the gardener takes care of the flowers to help them grow strong and healthy."

Leila thought about how wonderful it was that Allah took care of everything.

They reached a part of the garden where there were many butterflies flying around. The butterflies landed on the flowers, sipping nectar.

"Jadda, why do butterflies like flowers so much?" Leila asked.

"Butterflies need the nectar from flowers for food," her Jadda said. "And in return, they help the flowers by spreading pollen. This helps new flowers grow. Allah made everything in nature to work together perfectly."

Leila was amazed by how everything in nature was connected. She felt happy and peaceful in the garden, surrounded by the beauty of Allah's creation.

After a while, Leila and her Jadda sat down on a bench to rest.

"Jadda, I'm so glad we came to the garden today," Leila said. "I learned so much about flowers and how Allah created everything so beautifully."

Her Jadda hugged her and said, "I'm glad too, Leila. It's important to appreciate the beauty of Allah's creation and to remember that everything around us is a gift from Him."

As the sun began to set, Leila and her Jadda walked back home. Leila felt grateful for the wonderful day she had spent in the garden. That night, before going to bed, she whispered a prayer.

"Thank you, Allah, for the beautiful flowers and for showing me the wonders of Your creation. Please help me to always appreciate and take care of the world You have made."

Moral of the Story: The beauty of flowers reminds us of Allah's greatness and creativity. Each flower is unique and shows the love and care Allah put into creating the world.

Chapter 21

Allah's Majesty in Mountains

One bright morning, a little boy named Amir woke up with excitement. Today, his Jaddi had promised to take him on a hike to a nearby mountain. Amir had never climbed a mountain before, and he was very eager to see what it was like.

After breakfast, Amir and his Jaddi set off on their adventure. As they walked, Amir looked up at the tall mountain ahead of them. It seemed so big and strong. "Jaddi, why are mountains so tall and strong?" he asked.

His Jaddi smiled and said, "Allah created the mountains to be tall and strong. They remind us of His greatness and power. Mountains are also very important because they help keep the Earth stable."

Amir listened carefully as they continued walking. He thought about how amazing it was that Allah created everything with a purpose. As they got closer to the mountain, Amir saw beautiful flowers and trees growing along the path. Birds were singing in the trees, and the air smelled fresh and clean.

"Look, Jaddi! The flowers and trees are so beautiful," Amir said.

"Yes, Amir," his Jaddi replied. "Allah's creation is full of beauty. The mountains, trees, and flowers all show us the wonders of Allah's work."

They began to climb the mountain. The path was steep and rocky, but Amir was determined to reach the top. His Jaddi held his hand and helped him over the rough spots. "Remember, Amir, Allah gives us strength and courage. Whenever you feel tired, just ask Allah for help," he said.

As they climbed higher, Amir felt the wind blowing gently. It felt cool and refreshing on his face. He took a deep breath and felt grateful for the clean, fresh air. "Jaddi, I'm so glad we came on this hike. It's so beautiful up here," he said.

His Jaddi nodded. "Yes, Amir. Being in nature helps us feel closer to Allah. It reminds us of His greatness and the blessings He has given us."

Finally, they reached the top of the mountain. Amir looked around in awe. He could see the whole valley below, with rivers, trees, and houses. It was a breathtaking sight. "Subhan Allah, this is so amazing," Amir whispered.

His Jaddi smiled and said, "Yes, Amir. When we see such beauty, we should always remember to praise Allah. He created all of this for us to enjoy and to remind us of His power and love."

They sat down on a rock to rest and enjoy the view. Amir felt a sense of peace and happiness. He realized how small he was compared to the big, strong mountain and how great Allah's creation was.

As they made their way back down the mountain, Amir thought about everything he had seen and learned. He felt grateful for the experience and for the chance to see the greatness of Allah's creation up close.

That night, before going to bed, Amir whispered a prayer, "Thank you, Allah, for the beautiful mountain and for helping me reach the top. Please help me always remember your greatness and be grateful for your blessings."

Moral of the Story: Mountains, trees, and all of nature remind us of Allah's wonderful creation. Always remember to appreciate the beauty around you and thank Allah for His blessings. Allah gives us strength and courage to overcome challenges, just like climbing a mountain.

Chapter 22

Allah, The Bountiful

Once upon a time, in a small village, there lived a little boy named Ali. Ali was a kind and happy boy. He loved playing with his friends, going to school, and helping his parents. Every night before bed, Ali's Ummi would tell him stories about Allah, the Most Generous. She told Ali how Allah loves to give gifts to everyone.

One sunny morning, Ali woke up early. He looked out of his window and saw the bright sun shining. "Thank you, Allah, for the beautiful sunshine," Ali said with a big smile. He remembered what his Ummi told him: that everything around us is a gift from Allah.

Ali got ready and went to school. On his way, he saw a beautiful garden full of colorful flowers. The flowers were red, yellow, pink, and blue. They smelled so sweet. Ali stopped and picked a little flower to give to his teacher. "Thank you, Allah, for the lovely flowers," Ali said. He felt happy to share Allah's gifts.

At school, Ali's teacher, Miss Aisha, was very kind. She told the class about Allah's generosity. "Allah gives us so many things," she said. "The food we eat, the water we drink, the air we breathe, and even the love we feel in our hearts. Allah is very generous."

Ali listened carefully. He wanted to be like Allah, generous and kind. He decided to share his lunch with his friend, Sarah, who forgot to bring hers. "Here, Sarah, you can have some of my sandwich," Ali said. Sarah smiled and thanked him. Ali felt happy inside. He knew that sharing made Allah happy too.

After school, Ali and his friends went to the playground. They played games and laughed a lot. Ali noticed a little boy sitting alone. The boy looked sad. Ali walked over to him and said, "Hi, my name is Ali. Do you want to play with us?" The little boy nodded and smiled. "Thank you," he said softly. Ali felt good. He was glad to make a new friend and to share the fun.

When Ali got home, his Ummi was in the kitchen. She was cooking a delicious dinner. The smell of the food made Ali's tummy rumble. "Thank you, Allah, for the yummy food," Ali said. He remembered how lucky he was to have such a loving family and tasty meals. Ali helped his Ummi set the table. He wanted to show his gratitude by helping.

That evening, Ali's Abu came home with a big basket of fresh fruits. "Look what I brought for you, Ali!" his Abu said. The basket was full of apples, oranges, and bananas. Ali's eyes lit up with joy. "Thank you, Abu! And thank you, Allah, for the fruits," Ali said. He knew that Allah's generosity was endless.

Before bed, Ali sat with his Ummi again. She told him, "Ali, when we share what we have, we show that we are grateful for Allah's gifts. Allah loves it when we are kind and generous to others." Ali nodded. He understood now. Being generous made him and others happy.

As Ali lay in bed, he thought about all the wonderful things Allah gave him. He thought about the sunshine, flowers, food, friends, and family. Ali whispered, "Thank you, Allah, for everything. I will always try to be generous like You."

Moral of the Story: Sharing and being kind makes Allah happy and makes us feel good inside. Always be thankful for Allah's gifts.

Chapter 23

Allah's Nighttime Gift

One evening in a small village, a little boy named Hassan was playing outside with his friends. They ran and laughed, playing tag until the sky turned orange and the sun began to set. "Time to come inside, Hassan!" his Ummi called from the doorway.

Hassan waved goodbye to his friends and ran into the house. He loved playing with his friends, but he also loved the cozy time he spent with his family in the evening. After dinner, Hassan's Ummi asked him to get ready for bed.

"Okay, Ummi," Hassan said, yawning. He washed his face, brushed his teeth, and put on his pajamas. Then he went to his room and saw his Ummi waiting for him with a smile.

"Ummi, why do we have to sleep?" Hassan asked as he climbed into bed.

His Ummi tucked him in and said, "Allah has given us the gift of sleep to help our bodies rest and recharge. Just like you get tired after playing, your body needs sleep to feel strong and healthy again."

Hassan listened carefully. He knew that sleep was important, but he had never thought of it as a gift from Allah. "Ummi, can you tell me more about why sleep is a gift?" he asked.

His Ummi nodded. "When we sleep, our bodies rest and grow. Our minds get a chance to relax, and we wake up feeling fresh and ready for a new day. Sleep helps us stay healthy and happy."

Hassan's Ummi continued, "And before we sleep, we should always say our prayers and thank Allah for the day we've had. It's also good to say Bismillah before we close our eyes, asking Allah to protect us through the night."

Hassan folded his hands and said his evening prayers. "Thank you, Allah, for a wonderful day. Please give me a good night's sleep and help me wake up refreshed," he prayed. Then he added, "Bismillah," and closed his eyes.

As Hassan lay in bed, he thought about how wonderful sleep really was. He remembered how tired he felt after playing and how good it felt to rest. He thought about all the amazing things Allah had given him, like his family, friends, and a warm bed to sleep in.

The next morning, Hassan woke up feeling refreshed and happy. He stretched his arms and smiled. "Good morning, Ummi!" he called out as he ran to the kitchen.

"Good morning, Hassan," his Ummi said, giving him a big hug. "Did you sleep well?"

"Yes, Ummi," Hassan replied. "I feel great! Thank you, Allah, for the gift of sleep," he added with a grin.

His Ummi smiled and said, "See, Hassan? When we appreciate the gifts Allah gives us, we feel happier and more thankful."

Hassan nodded. He decided to always remember to thank Allah for the gift of sleep and to say his prayers before bed. He knew that sleep was important for his body and mind, and he felt grateful for this special gift from Allah.

That evening, as Hassan got ready for bed again, he felt a warm and peaceful feeling in his heart. He said his prayers, thanked Allah for the day, and whispered, "Bismillah," before closing his eyes.

Moral of the Story: Sleep is a precious gift from Allah. It helps our bodies rest and our minds relax so we can wake up feeling fresh and happy. Always remember to thank Allah for the gift of sleep and to say your prayers before bed. Being grateful for Allah's gifts makes us happier and more peaceful.

Chapter 24

Allah's Gift of Life

Once upon a time, in a small village, there lived a little girl named Aisha. Aisha was a curious and happy girl. She loved playing with her friends, going to school, and helping her parents. One day, Aisha's Ummi told her that soon there would be a new baby in their family. Aisha was very excited. She couldn't wait to meet her new baby brother or sister.

Aisha's Ummi explained, "Aisha, every new life is a miracle from Allah. Allah creates every baby and gives them life." Aisha listened carefully. She wanted to know more about this miracle.

One sunny morning, Aisha and her Ummi went to visit their neighbor, who had just had a baby. When they arrived, Aisha saw the tiny baby sleeping in a crib. The baby had soft skin and tiny fingers and toes. Aisha's Ummi said, "Look, Aisha, this baby is a gift from Allah. Allah made this baby special and unique."

Aisha gently touched the baby's hand. The baby's fingers curled around Aisha's finger. Aisha smiled and felt very happy. She whispered, "Thank you, Allah, for this beautiful baby."

As they walked home, Aisha's Ummi told her more about the miracle of birth. "Aisha, every baby starts as a tiny seed in the mother's tummy. Allah makes the baby grow little by little until it is ready to be born."

Aisha thought this was amazing. She couldn't believe that such a small seed could become a wonderful baby.

A few months later, Aisha's family went to the hospital. Her Ummi was ready to have the new baby. Aisha waited with her Abu, feeling excited and a little nervous. After a while, a nurse came out and said, "Congratulations! You have a new baby brother." Aisha's heart filled with joy.

When Aisha saw her baby brother for the first time, she felt a warm, happy feeling in her heart. The baby was tiny and cute, with big brown eyes and a little button nose. Aisha's Ummi smiled and said, "Aisha, this is your baby brother. He is a miracle from Allah."

Aisha gently kissed her baby brother on the forehead. She felt very thankful for this precious gift. "Welcome to our family, little brother," Aisha whispered. She knew that Allah had blessed their family with this wonderful baby.

At home, Aisha loved helping her Ummi take care of the baby. She would sing lullabies, help change diapers, and even rock the baby to sleep. Every time she looked at her baby brother, she remembered that he was a miracle from Allah.

One evening, Aisha's Abu gathered the family together. He said, "Aisha, we are so proud of you for being such a good sister. Always remember that every new life is a special gift from Allah. We should always be thankful for these miracles."

Aisha nodded and smiled. She understood now how special her baby brother was. She felt grateful for Allah's wonderful gift. That night, as she lay in bed, Aisha whispered, "Thank you, Allah, for my baby brother. Thank you for the miracle of life."

Moral of the Story: Every new life is a special miracle from Allah. Always be thankful for these precious gifts.

Chapter 25

Allah, The Life Sustainer

One bright morning, a little boy named Ali woke up with a big smile. He was excited because he was going to visit his Jaddi's farm. Ali loved going to the farm because he got to see all the animals and plants.

After breakfast, Ali and his Abu set off for the farm. When they arrived, Ali saw his Jaddi feeding the chickens. "Assalamu Alaikum, Jaddi!" Ali called out.

"Wa Alaikum Assalam, Ali," Jaddi replied. "Are you ready to help me on the farm today?"

"Yes, Jaddi! I can't wait," Ali said eagerly.

They walked to the vegetable garden first. Ali saw rows of tomatoes, cucumbers, and carrots. "Look at all these vegetables, Jaddi!" Ali exclaimed.

"Yes, Ali," Jaddi said. "Allah is Ar-Razzaq, the Sustainer. He provides everything we need, like these vegetables. They grow because Allah gives them sunlight, water, and good soil."

Ali nodded, thinking about how Allah makes the plants grow. He helped his Jaddi water the plants and felt grateful for the fresh vegetables.

Next, they went to the barn where the cows were. Jaddi showed Ali how to milk a cow. "The cows give us milk, and we use it to make cheese, butter, and yogurt," Jaddi explained.

"Alhamdulillah, for the milk," Ali said. He realized how Allah provides food for them through the animals.

As they walked around the farm, Ali saw birds flying and singing in the trees. "Jaddi, why do the birds sing?" Ali asked.

"The birds sing to praise Allah," Jaddi said. "Allah gives them food and places to live. He takes care of all His creatures."

Ali smiled, feeling happy to hear the birds' songs. He knew that Allah was taking care of everything.

They walked to a small pond where ducks were swimming. Ali watched the ducks and said, "Jaddi, the ducks look so happy in the water."

"Yes, Ali," Jaddi replied. "Allah provides the water for them to swim in and the food they eat. Allah is always taking care of us and all the animals."

After a busy day on the farm, Ali and his Abu thanked Jaddi and headed back home. Ali felt grateful for everything he had seen and learned. "Thank you, Allah, for providing everything we need," he whispered.

That evening, Ali helped his Ummi prepare dinner. He thought about the vegetables from the garden and the milk from the cows. He felt happy knowing that Allah was always providing for them.

Before going to bed, Ali said his prayers, "Thank you, Allah, for being our Sustainer. Thank you for the food, water, and everything you give us. Please help us always remember to be grateful."

Ali felt peaceful and happy as he drifted off to sleep. He knew that Allah was always there to take care of him and his family.

Moral of the Story: Allah is Ar-Razzaq, the Sustainer. He provides us with everything we need to live. Always be thankful for Allah's blessings and remember that He is always taking care of us.

Chapter 26

Allah's Colorful Creation

Once upon a time, in a small village, there lived a little girl named Noor. Noor loved to explore and discover new things. She was always curious about the world around her. One day, her Jadda told her that the beautiful colors in nature are a sign of Allah's creativity.

One sunny morning, Noor and her Jadda went for a walk in the village. The sky was bright blue, and the sun was shining. Noor looked up and said, "Jadda, the sky is so blue today! It's so pretty." Her Jadda smiled and said, "Yes, Noor. Allah made the sky blue to show us His creativity."

As they walked, they came to a garden full of flowers. There were red roses, yellow sunflowers, pink tulips, and purple lilacs. Noor's eyes widened with wonder. "Look at all the beautiful colors, Jadda!" she exclaimed. Her Jadda said, "Allah created these flowers in many different colors to make the world beautiful."

Noor gently touched a red rose. She smelled its sweet fragrance and felt happy. "Thank you, Allah, for these lovely flowers," she whispered. Noor and her Jadda continued their walk and saw a butterfly with colorful wings. The butterfly had orange, black, and white patterns. It fluttered around the flowers, making Noor smile.

"Jadda, the butterfly is so colorful!" Noor said. Her Jadda nodded and said, "Yes, Noor. Allah made the butterfly's wings colorful to show us His wonderful creativity. Each butterfly is unique and special."

They walked further and saw a big, green tree. The leaves rustled in the gentle breeze. Noor's Jadda said, "Allah made the trees green to give us shade and fresh air. The green leaves are a sign of Allah's care for us."

As they walked through the fields, Noor noticed the golden wheat swaying in the wind. "Jadda, the wheat is so shiny and gold!" Noor said. Her Jadda replied, "Allah made the wheat golden so we can see its beauty and be thankful for our food."

Noor saw a rainbow in the sky. It had red, orange, yellow, green, blue, and purple colors. Noor was amazed. "Jadda, look at the rainbow! It's so beautiful!" she exclaimed. Her Jadda smiled and said, "Yes, Noor. The rainbow is one of Allah's most beautiful creations. It shows us all the colors of the world in one place."

As they walked back home, Noor saw a little bird with bright blue feathers and a yellow beak. The bird was singing a sweet song. "Jadda, the bird is so colorful and happy!" Noor said. Her Jadda replied,

"Allah gave the bird its colors and song to make the world joyful and beautiful."

At home, Noor helped her Jadda in the garden. They planted seeds and watered the plants. Noor felt grateful for all the beautiful colors in the world. "Thank you, Allah, for the flowers, the trees, the butterflies, and all the colors," she said with a big smile.

That evening, Noor sat with her family and shared what she had learned. "Today, Jadda and I saw so many beautiful colors in nature. Allah made everything so colorful to show us His creativity," she said. Her parents smiled and nodded.

As Noor got ready for bed, she felt happy and peaceful. She knew that Allah's creativity was all around her, in every color of the world. Noor whispered, "Thank you, Allah, for making the world so beautiful," before closing her eyes and drifting off to sleep.

Moral of the Story: The beautiful colors in nature remind us of Allah's creativity. Always be thankful for Allah's wonderful creations.

Chapter 27

Allah's Blessing of Friends

Once upon a time, in a small village, there lived a little girl named Amina. Amina was a cheerful and kind-hearted girl. She loved playing with her friends and helping her family. She lived with her parents and her younger brother, Ali, in a cozy house with a beautiful garden.

One day, Amina's best friend, Sara, told her some sad news. "Amina, I am moving to a new city. My dad got a new job there," Sara said with tears in her eyes.

Amina felt her heart sink. Sara was her best friend, and they did everything together. "When are you leaving?" Amina asked, trying to hold back her tears.

"In a week," Sara replied. They hugged each other tightly, feeling very sad.

The days passed quickly, and soon it was time for Sara to leave. Amina and Sara hugged one last time and said goodbye. Amina felt very lonely without Sara. She missed playing games, sharing stories, and laughing together.

One evening, Amina's Ummi noticed that Amina was very quiet and not her usual happy self. "Amina, what's wrong?" she asked gently.

"I miss Sara so much, Ummi. I feel so sad," Amina replied, tears rolling down her cheeks.

Amina's Ummi hugged her and said, "It's okay to feel sad, my dear. Remember, Allah is always with us, especially when we feel sad. He comforts us and helps us feel better."

Amina listened carefully as her Ummi continued, "When we feel sad, we can pray to Allah and tell Him how we feel. He listens to our prayers and gives us comfort."

That night, Amina prayed to Allah. She closed her eyes and said, "Dear Allah, I feel very sad because my friend Sara moved away. Please help me feel better and find new friends to play with."

The next morning, Amina felt a little better. She decided to visit the village park. There, she saw a new girl sitting alone on a bench. Amina remembered what her Ummi said about being kind and making new friends.

Amina walked up to the girl and said, "Hi, my name is Amina. What's your name?"

The girl looked up and smiled. "Hi, Amina. My name is Fatima. I just moved here and I don't know anyone yet."

Amina felt a warm feeling in her heart. "Would you like to play with me?" she asked.

Fatima's face lit up with joy. "Yes, I would love to!" she replied.

Amina and Fatima played together in the park. They laughed, ran around, and had a lot of fun. Amina felt happy again. She knew that Allah had listened to her prayers and helped her find a new friend.

From that day on, Amina and Fatima became best friends. They played together every day, shared stories, and helped each other. Amina still missed Sara, but she knew that Allah was always there to comfort her and bring new friends into her life.

That night, as she lay in bed, Amina whispered, "Thank you, Allah, for helping me find a new friend. Thank you for always being there for me."

Moral of the Story: When we feel sad, we can pray to Allah for comfort. He listens to our prayers and helps us feel better. Always remember that Allah is with us, especially in times of sadness.

Chapter 28

Allah's Happiness in Smiles

Once upon a time, in a small village, there lived a little girl named Maryam. Maryam was known for her bright smile that made everyone around her feel happy. She loved spreading joy and making others smile.

One sunny morning, Maryam woke up with a big smile on her face. She said, "Bismillah," before starting her day. After breakfast, she went outside to play with her friends. As she was playing, she saw her neighbor, Mrs. Amina, who looked very sad.

"Assalamu Alaikum, Mrs. Amina," Maryam said with a smile. "Are you okay?"

"Wa Alaikum Assalam, Maryam," Mrs. Amina replied. "I am feeling a bit sad today."

Maryam thought for a moment and decided to do something to cheer her up. She ran home and quickly drew a beautiful picture of a sunny day with flowers and birds. She wrote, "May Allah bless your day with happiness," on the picture. Then she took it to Mrs. Amina.

"Here, Mrs. Amina, I made this for you," Maryam said, handing her the picture.

Mrs. Amina's face lit up with a smile. "Thank you so much, Maryam. This is very kind of you."

Seeing Mrs. Amina smile made Maryam feel very happy. She knew that Allah loves those who spread joy and kindness. As she walked back home, she whispered, "Alhamdulillah," for the chance to make someone happy.

Later that day, Maryam saw her little brother, Ali, looking upset because he had lost his favorite toy. Maryam went to him and said, "Don't worry, Ali. Let's look for it together."

They searched the house and finally found the toy under the couch. Ali's face beamed with joy. "Thank you, Maryam! You're the best Ukhti ever!"

Maryam felt her heart fill with warmth. She loved seeing her Khuya happy and knew that Allah was pleased with her for helping others.

Maryam felt a sense of accomplishment and joy. She loved helping her family and making them happy. She whispered, "Alhamdulillah," for the opportunity to help.

That evening, as Maryam got ready for bed, she thought about all the smiles she had seen that day. She felt happy and peaceful knowing that she had spread joy and kindness.

Maryam said her prayers and thanked Allah for a wonderful day. "Thank you, Allah, for letting me make others smile today. Please help me to always be kind and spread happiness."

As she drifted off to sleep, Maryam knew that the gift of smiles was one of the most beautiful gifts from Allah.

Moral of the Story: Spreading joy and kindness through smiles makes Allah happy and brings happiness to others. Always be thankful for the opportunity to make others smile and remember that a simple act of kindness can brighten someone's day.

Chapter 29

Allah's Gift of Ears

Once upon a time, in a small village, there was a little boy named Ali. Ali was six years old and loved to play outside with his friends. He liked to listen to the birds singing and the wind blowing through the trees. Ali knew that hearing was a special gift from Allah.

One sunny day, Ali went to the park with his friends, Amina, Hassan, and Sara. They played tag, ran around, and laughed a lot. Ali felt happy when he heard his friends laughing and calling his name. He knew that hearing their voices made him feel loved and cared for.

Ali's teacher, Ms. Fatima, taught the children about the five senses: sight, smell, taste, touch, and hearing. She told them that hearing helps us enjoy beautiful sounds like music, birds, and the voices of our loved ones. Ms. Fatima said that Allah gave us hearing as a special gift so we can learn and be safe.

Ali remembered what Ms. Fatima had said one afternoon when he was at home. His Ummi was cooking in the kitchen, and the delicious smell of food filled the house. Ali heard the sound of the knife chopping vegetables and the sizzle of food in the pan. He went to the kitchen and asked his Ummi, "Yumma, can I help you cook?"

His Ummi smiled and said, "Of course, Ali! Thank you for asking." She showed him how to mix the salad and stir the soup. Ali listened carefully to his Ummi's instructions. He knew that hearing helped him learn how to cook.

One night, there was a big storm. The wind howled, and the rain pounded on the roof. Ali felt scared and covered his ears. His Abu came and sat beside him, hugging him tightly. "Don't worry, Ali," his Abu said softly. "We are safe inside our home. Allah is protecting us."

Ali felt better when he heard his Abu's comforting words. He realized that hearing can also help us feel safe and calm.

The next day, Ali went to school and told his friends about the storm. Hassan said, "I was scared too, but my Ummi sang me a lullaby, and I felt better."

Amina added, "My Abu read me a story. Hearing his voice made me feel safe."

Sara said, "My Khuya told me a funny joke, and I laughed. It helped me forget about the storm."

Ali and his friends understood that hearing kind words and songs can make us feel happy and safe. They thanked Allah for the gift of hearing.

One day, Ms. Fatima took the class to visit a special place called the Hearing Center. They met people who could not hear well. The children learned that some people need hearing aids to help them hear. They also learned a little sign language to talk to people who are deaf.

Ali was amazed. He saw how important hearing is and how it helps us communicate. He felt thankful for his ability to hear.

As Ali grew older, he always remembered to thank Allah for the gift of hearing. He listened to the sounds around him with a happy heart. He enjoyed the songs of birds, the laughter of friends, and the loving words of his family. Ali knew that hearing was a wonderful gift from Allah.

Moral of the Story: Hearing is a special gift from Allah. It helps us learn, stay safe, and feel happy. Always be thankful for your ability to hear.

Chapter 30

Allah's Lesson in Sharing

Once upon a time, in a small village, there lived a little girl named Zainab. Zainab was seven years old and loved to play with her friends. She had a big smile and a kind heart. Zainab knew that giving and sharing were important lessons from Allah.

One bright morning, Zainab went to the park with her friends, Omar, Layla, and Samir. They played games and had lots of fun. Zainab had brought a basket of fresh apples with her. Her Ummi had picked them from their apple tree.

As they were playing, Omar said, "I'm feeling very thirsty and a little hungry." Zainab remembered the apples in her basket. She smiled and said, "Omar, I have some apples. Would you like one?"

Omar's eyes lit up. "Yes, please!" he said. Zainab gave Omar a big, red apple. Omar took a bite and said, "Thank you, Zainab. This apple is delicious!"

Seeing Omar happy made Zainab feel good. She then offered apples to Layla and Samir. They both smiled and took the apples happily. "Thank you, Zainab," they said together.

While they were eating, Zainab told her friends, "My Ummi says that Allah loves it when we give and share with others. It makes our hearts kind and our souls happy."

Layla nodded and said, "My Baba told me the same thing. He said that when we share, we show love and care for each other."

Just then, a little boy named Ahmed walked by. Ahmed was new to the village and didn't have many friends yet. He watched the children playing and eating apples. Zainab noticed Ahmed and waved to him. "Hi, Ahmed! Would you like to join us and have an apple?"

Ahmed's face brightened up. "Really? Can I?" he asked shyly.

"Of course!" Zainab said, handing him an apple. Ahmed sat down with the group and took a bite. "This is so tasty! Thank you, Zainab."

Zainab smiled and said, "We are happy to share with you, Ahmed. You are our friend."

After they finished their apples, the children played more games together. They laughed and had a wonderful time. Ahmed felt so happy to be included and make new friends.

Later that evening, Zainab went home and told her Ummi about the fun day at the park. She also told her about sharing the apples with her friends and Ahmed. Her Ummi hugged her and said, "Zainab, I am so proud of you. Allah teaches us to give and share with others. You have a kind heart."

The next day at school, Zainab saw a girl named Fatima who looked sad. Zainab went to her and asked, "What's wrong, Fatima?"

Fatima sighed and said, "I forgot my lunch at home today."

Zainab quickly opened her lunchbox. She had a sandwich, some grapes, and a cookie. "Don't worry, Fatima. You can share my lunch," Zainab said.

Fatima smiled and said, "Thank you, Zainab. You are very kind."

Zainab felt happy again. She knew that sharing her lunch was the right thing to do. She thanked Allah for the lesson and promised to always share what she had with others.

Moral of the Story: Giving and sharing make our hearts kind and our souls happy. Always remember to share what you have with others.

Chapter 31

Allah's Help in Hard Times

Once upon a time, in a small village, there was a boy named Yusuf. Yusuf loved to play with his friends. He had a big smile and a brave heart. Yusuf knew that Allah was always there to help him, especially in difficult times.

One day, Yusuf and his friends, Aisha, Bilal, and Fatima, decided to go on a little adventure. They wanted to explore the forest near their village. Yusuf's Ummi reminded him, "Remember, Yusuf, always ask Allah for help when you need it." Yusuf nodded and promised to remember her words.

As the children entered the forest, they saw many beautiful trees, colorful flowers, and heard birds singing. They walked and played, enjoying the beauty of nature. Suddenly, they heard a loud noise. It was a thunderstorm!

Dark clouds covered the sky, and it started to rain heavily. The children were scared and didn't know what to do. Yusuf remembered his Ummi's words and said, "Let's ask Allah for help."

The children closed their eyes and prayed, "Dear Allah, please help us find a safe place to stay until the storm passes." After their prayer, they opened their eyes and saw a small cave nearby. They quickly ran to the cave and took shelter inside.

Inside the cave, the children felt safe. They hugged each other and waited for the storm to end. Yusuf said, "See, Allah heard our prayer and helped us find this cave."

After a while, the rain stopped, and the sun came out. The children thanked Allah for keeping them safe. They carefully walked back to their village, feeling grateful for Allah's help.

Another day, Yusuf's Baba was working in the field. He was plowing the land to plant seeds. Suddenly, his tractor got stuck in the mud. Yusuf's Baba tried hard to pull it out, but it was too difficult. He felt tired and worried.

Yusuf saw his Baba struggling and ran to help him. "Don't worry, Baba," Yusuf said. "Let's ask Allah for help." They both prayed, "Dear Allah, please help us get the tractor out of the mud."

After their prayer, a strong man from the village named Ali walked by. He saw Yusuf and his Baba and came to help. With Ali's strength and their combined efforts, they were able to pull the tractor out of the mud.

Yusuf's Baba smiled and said, "Thank you, Ali. And thank you, Yusuf, for reminding me to ask Allah for help." Yusuf felt happy knowing that Allah had sent Ali to help them.

One evening, Fatima, Yusuf's Ikht, was doing her homework. She had a difficult math problem and didn't know how to solve it. She felt frustrated and sad. Yusuf saw her and said, "Don't worry, Fatima. Let's ask Allah for help."

They prayed together, "Dear Allah, please help Fatima understand her math problem." After their prayer, Yusuf sat with Fatima and tried to explain the problem to her. With patience and effort, Fatima finally understood and solved the problem.

Fatima hugged Yusuf and said, "Thank you, Yusuf. And thank you, Allah, for helping me." Yusuf felt proud of his sister and thankful to Allah.

From that day on, Yusuf and his friends always remembered to ask Allah for help in difficult times. They knew that Allah was always there to guide and support them.

Moral of the Story: Allah helps us in difficult times. Always remember to pray and ask for His help when you need it.

Chapter 32

Allah's Love in Family

Once upon a time, in a small village, there lived a little boy named Ahmed. Ahmed was seven years old and loved spending time with his family. He knew that family was a special blessing from Allah.

One sunny morning, Ahmed woke up and said, "Bismillah," as he started his day. He greeted his Ummi, "Assalamu Alaikum, Ummi!"

"Wa Alaikum Assalam, Ahmed," his Ummi replied with a warm smile. "Today, we are going to visit Jaddi and Jaddati. They have been looking forward to seeing you."

Ahmed felt excited. He loved spending time with his grandparents. After breakfast, they got ready and left for Jaddi and Jaddati's house. When they arrived, Jaddi was in the garden, and Jaddati was in the kitchen.

"Assalamu Alaikum, Jaddi and Jaddati!" Ahmed called out cheerfully.

"Wa Alaikum Assalam, Ahmed!" Jaddi and Jaddati replied, their faces lighting up with joy.

Ahmed ran to Jaddi, who was tending to the plants. "Jaddi, can I help you in the garden?" Ahmed asked eagerly.

"Of course, Ahmed," Jaddi said, handing him a small watering can. "Let's water the plants together. These plants need care just like we do."

As they watered the plants, Jaddi explained how Allah created everything and how it is our duty to take care of Allah's creations. Ahmed listened carefully and felt grateful for the lessons from his Jaddi.

After helping in the garden, Ahmed went inside to see his Jaddati. The kitchen smelled wonderful. "What are you cooking, Jaddati?" Ahmed asked.

"I am making your favorite, Ahmed. It's a special treat for you," Jaddati replied with a loving smile. "Would you like to help me?"

"Yes, please!" Ahmed said excitedly. He washed his hands and helped Jaddati mix the ingredients. He loved spending time with his Jaddati and learning how to cook.

When the food was ready, they all sat down together to eat. "Bismillah," they said before starting their meal. The food tasted even better because they were enjoying it together.

After lunch, Ahmed's Abu told them a wonderful plan. "Let's all go to the park this afternoon," he said. Everyone agreed happily.

At the park, Ahmed played with his Akhi and Ukhti. They ran around, played games, and laughed a lot. Ahmed's Baba watched them and felt grateful for the happiness in his family.

In the evening, as the sun was setting, they all sat together under a big tree. Ahmed's Ummi shared stories about their family and how Allah had blessed them with love and togetherness. Ahmed listened intently, feeling thankful for his wonderful family.

When they returned home, Ahmed felt very happy and peaceful. He loved spending the day with his family. Before going to bed, he said his prayers. "Thank you, Allah, for my family. Thank you for Jaddi, Jaddati, Ummi, Abu, Akhi, and Ukhti. Please keep us all safe and happy."

Ahmed fell asleep with a big smile on his face, knowing that his family was a precious gift from Allah. He promised himself to always cherish and care for them.

Moral of the Story: Family is a special blessing from Allah. Always be thankful for your family, love them, and take care of them. They are a precious gift that brings happiness and joy to our lives.

Chapter 33

Alhamdulillah: Thanking Allah

Once upon a time, in a small village, there was a little boy named Hassan. Hassan loved playing with his friends. He had a big smile and a kind heart. Although Hassan knew that saying "Alhamdulillah" was important, he often forgot to say it.

One sunny morning, Hassan woke up and said, "Bismillah," as he started his day. He greeted his Ummi, "Assalamu Alaikum, Ummi!"

"Wa Alaikum Assalam, Hassan," his Ummi replied with a warm smile. "Today is a beautiful day. Let's be thankful and say 'Alhamdulillah' for all the blessings we have."

Hassan smiled and nodded but didn't say "Alhamdulillah." After breakfast, Hassan went outside to play with his friends, Ali, Layla, and Amina. They played games, ran around, and laughed a lot. Hassan felt happy to have such wonderful friends.

During their playtime, Hassan tripped and fell. He scraped his knee and felt a little pain. Ali ran over to help him up. "Are you okay, Hassan?" he asked.

Hassan nodded, wiping away his tears. "Yes, I'm okay," he said, forgetting to say "Alhamdulillah."

After playing, the children sat down under a big tree to rest. Layla took out some cookies her Jadda had made. She shared them with everyone. "Bismillah," they all said before eating.

The cookies were delicious, and Hassan felt grateful but forgot to say "Alhamdulillah." "These cookies are so tasty. Thank you, Layla," he said.

In the afternoon, Hassan went home to help his Baba in the garden. They planted flowers and watered the plants together. Hassan enjoyed spending time with his Baba and learning how to take care of the garden.

"Baba, the garden looks so beautiful," Hassan said.

"Yes, Hassan. Allah has given us this beautiful garden," his Baba replied.

That evening, Hassan's family gathered for dinner. His Ummi had cooked a delicious meal. They all said, "Bismillah," before starting to eat. Hassan enjoyed the food and felt thankful for his family but again forgot to say "Alhamdulillah."

After dinner, Hassan's Akhi, Yusuf, showed him a new toy he had made from some old materials. "Look, Hassan! I made this for you," Yusuf said.

Hassan was delighted. "Thank you, Akhi! I have such a kind brother," he said, giving Yusuf a big hug but still didn't say "Alhamdulillah."

Before going to bed, Hassan sat with his Jaddi. His Jaddi told him, "Hassan, do you know the importance of saying 'Alhamdulillah'? It means 'All praise is due to Allah.' It reminds us to be grateful for all the blessings Allah has given us, big and small."

Hassan listened carefully. "Why is it so important, Jaddi?" he asked.

"When we say 'Alhamdulillah,' it makes our hearts happy and thankful. It helps us remember that Allah provides for us and takes care of us. Being grateful brings more blessings into our lives," his Jaddi explained.

Hassan thought about this. He realized that he had not been saying "Alhamdulillah" as much as he should. He promised himself to start saying it more often.

That night, Hassan whispered a prayer, "Thank you, Allah, for my family, my friends, and all the blessings you have given me. Alhamdulillah."

The next day, Hassan woke up and said, "Bismillah" and "Alhamdulillah" for the new day. He felt a sense of peace and happiness. At breakfast, he remembered to say "Alhamdulillah" for the food.

When he went outside to play with his friends, he said "Alhamdulillah" for the sunny day. When he tripped and fell, he said "Alhamdulillah" for not getting seriously hurt. His friends noticed how happy and thankful he seemed.

"Hassan, you're saying 'Alhamdulillah' a lot today," Layla observed.

"Yes," Hassan replied. "I've learned that saying 'Alhamdulillah' makes me feel happy and grateful. It helps me remember that Allah is always taking care of us."

From that day on, Hassan made sure to say "Alhamdulillah" often. He noticed that he felt happier and more at peace. He knew that being grateful to Allah brought blessings into his life and made his heart feel full of joy.

Moral of the Story: Always remember to say "Alhamdulillah" for all the blessings in your life. Being thankful to Allah makes your heart happy and helps you appreciate everything you have.

Chapter 34

Allah's Cycle of Night and Day

Once upon a time, in a small village, there was a little boy named Hassan. Hassan was curious about many things, especially the world around him. He loved asking his Ummi and Baba questions about everything he saw.

One morning, Hassan woke up early. The sun was shining, and the birds were singing. He ran to the kitchen and greeted his mother, "Assalamu Alaikum, Ummi!"

"Wa Alaikum Assalam, Hassan," his Ummi replied with a smile. "You are up early today!"

"Yes, Ummi! I love the mornings. The sun is so bright and warm," Hassan said happily. "Why does the sun come up every day?"

"Allah created the sun to give us light and warmth during the day," his Ummi explained. "The day is for us to work, play, and enjoy Allah's blessings."

Hassan thought about this as he ate his breakfast. Afterward, he went outside to play with his friends, Bilal, Layla, and Ali. They ran around, played games, and enjoyed the beautiful sunny day. Hassan felt happy and thankful for the sunshine.

As the day went on, Hassan noticed the sun slowly moving down the sky. Soon, it started to get dark. He ran back home and found his Baba reading a book. "Assalamu Alaikum, Baba!" he called out.

"Wa Alaikum Assalam, Hassan," his Baba replied, putting his book down. "How was your day?"

"It was wonderful, Baba. But now it's getting dark. Why does the sun go away?" Hassan asked.

"The sun sets so that night can come," his Baba said. "Allah created the night for us to rest and sleep. Just as the day is important for activity, the night is important for rest."

Hassan nodded, trying to understand. He spent the evening with his family, eating dinner and listening to his Jaddi's stories. As bedtime approached, he noticed the sky was filled with stars and the moon was shining brightly.

"Look, Baba! The moon and stars are so beautiful," Hassan said, pointing out the window.

"Yes, Hassan. Allah created the moon and stars to light up the night sky," his Baba explained. "The night is a time of peace and quiet. It helps us rest and recharge for the next day."

Before going to bed, Hassan said his evening prayers and thanked Allah for the day. "Thank you, Allah, for the beautiful day and the peaceful night," he whispered.

The next morning, Hassan woke up again to the bright sunshine. He felt rested and ready for another day of fun and learning. He went to the kitchen and greeted his Ummi, "Assalamu Alaikum, Ummi!"

"Wa Alaikum Assalam, Hassan," his Ummi replied. "Did you sleep well?"

"Yes, Ummi. I feel great! Alhamdulillah for the night and day," Hassan said with a big smile.

His Ummi hugged him and said, "Alhamdulillah indeed. Allah has given us the perfect balance of day and night to live happily and healthily."

As Hassan went about his day, he remembered to thank Allah for the sunshine that warmed him and the night that helped him rest. He realized that both the day and the night were special gifts from Allah.

Moral of the Story: Allah has created the day and night for us to live a balanced and healthy life. Always be thankful for the blessings of both the day and night.

Chapter 35

The First Salah: Allah's Gift

THE FIRST SALAH: ALLAH'S GIFT

Once upon a time, in a small village, there was a little boy named Ibrahim. Ibrahim was seven years old and loved playing with his friends. He lived with his Ummi and Baba. Ibrahim was always curious and eager to learn new things.

One day, Ibrahim's Jaddi came to visit. Jaddi was very wise and loved to teach Ibrahim about Islam. After lunch, Jaddi called Ibrahim to sit with him. "Assalamu Alaikum, my dear grandson," Jaddi greeted him.

"Wa Alaikum Assalam, Jaddi," Ibrahim replied.

"Ibrahim, do you know why it is important to pray?" Jaddi asked.

Ibrahim shook his head. "No, Jaddi. Can you tell me?"

"Of course," Jaddi replied with a smile. "Prayer is a special way to talk to Allah. It helps us stay close to Him and remember His blessings."

Ibrahim listened carefully. He wanted to learn how to pray. Jaddi explained the steps of the prayer and showed Ibrahim how to perform wudu, the washing before prayer. "Bismillah," Jaddi said as he washed his hands. Ibrahim watched closely and repeated after him.

Later that evening, it was time for Maghrib prayer. Jaddi called Ibrahim to join him. "Come, Ibrahim. Let's pray together."

Ibrahim felt a little nervous but excited. He stood next to his Jaddi and followed his movements. They said "Allahu Akbar" and began the prayer. Ibrahim tried his best to remember the steps and words.

After the prayer, Ibrahim felt very happy. "Alhamdulillah, I prayed for the first time!" he exclaimed.

"Alhamdulillah, Ibrahim," Jaddi said, smiling. "You did very well. Remember, prayer is a way to thank Allah for everything He has given us."

The next day, Ibrahim wanted to practice his prayer again. He asked his Baba to help him. "Baba, can you pray with me?"

"Of course, Ibrahim," Baba replied. "Let's say our prayers together."

Ibrahim and Baba prayed together, and Ibrahim felt more confident. He remembered to say "Bismillah" before starting and "Alhamdulillah" after finishing. Baba hugged Ibrahim and said, "I'm proud of you, Ibrahim. Always remember to pray and thank Allah."

As days passed, Ibrahim continued to pray with his family. He prayed with his Ummi and Baba, feeling closer to Allah and happy knowing he was doing something important.

One evening, Ibrahim's friend Bilal came to visit. Bilal saw Ibrahim praying and asked, "Ibrahim, can you teach me how to pray too?"

Ibrahim was thrilled. "Yes, Bilal! Come, I'll show you." Ibrahim taught Bilal how to perform wudu and the steps of the prayer. They prayed together, and Bilal felt happy to learn something new.

That night, Ibrahim sat with his family and said, "Alhamdulillah, I'm grateful for learning how to pray. Thank you, Jaddi, for teaching me."

"You're welcome, Ibrahim," Jaddi replied. "Remember, prayer is a gift from Allah. It brings us closer to Him and helps us remember His blessings."

Before going to bed, Ibrahim whispered a prayer, "Alhamdulillah, Allah, for helping me learn how to pray. Please guide me to always remember to pray and be thankful."

Moral of the Story: Prayer is a special way to talk to Allah and stay close to Him. It helps us remember His blessings and be thankful. Always remember to pray and thank Allah for everything.

Chapter 36

Eid: Allah's Festival of Joy

Once upon a time, in a small village, there lived a little boy named Yusuf. Yusuf was very excited because tomorrow was Eid, a special day of celebration for Muslims. He lived with his Ummi, Baba, and his younger brother, Akhi Bilal. The night before Eid, Yusuf helped his Ummi and Baba with the preparations.

"Assalamu Alaikum, Ummi! What can I do to help?" Yusuf asked.

"Wa Alaikum Assalam, Yusuf," his Ummi replied with a smile. "You can help me by arranging the sweets on the tray."

"Okay, Ummi," Yusuf said cheerfully. He carefully placed the sweets on the tray, making sure everything looked perfect.

The next morning, Yusuf woke up early. He said, "Bismillah," and got ready in his new clothes. He felt very happy and couldn't wait to go to the mosque with his Baba and Akhi Bilal for the special Eid prayer.

"Assalamu Alaikum, Baba! Are you ready for the Eid prayer?" Yusuf asked.

"Wa Alaikum Assalam, Yusuf. Yes, let's go," Baba replied.

They walked to the mosque, and Yusuf saw many people dressed in their best clothes. Everyone greeted each other with "Eid Mubarak!"

and big smiles. After the prayer, they hugged and wished each other happiness.

"Eid Mubarak, Baba!" Yusuf said, hugging his father.

"Eid Mubarak, Yusuf!" Baba replied, smiling warmly.

After the prayer, Baba explained, "Today is Eid al-Fitr, which comes after the holy month of Ramadan. During Ramadan, we fast from dawn to sunset to learn self-discipline and empathy for those in need. On Eid al-Fitr, we celebrate the end of Ramadan and thank Allah for the strength He gave us. The special prayer we performed at the mosque is called Salat al-Eid. It is a way to start the day with gratitude and remember Allah's blessings."

When they returned home, the house was filled with the delicious smell of food. Ummi and Jaddati had prepared a big feast. There were dishes like biryani, kebabs, and many kinds of sweets. Yusuf's mouth watered just smelling the food.

"Alhamdulillah for this wonderful feast," Yusuf said happily.

At the table, the family gathered and thanked Allah for all the blessings they had. Yusuf's Baba said, "Bismillah," before they started eating. They all enjoyed the meal together, laughing and talking about their favorite moments. Ummi explained, "We give sweets on Eid to share our happiness with others. It is a tradition that brings joy and sweetness to our hearts."

After the meal, Yusuf and Akhi Bilal went outside to play with their friends. The village was filled with joy and laughter. There were games, and everyone shared their sweets and treats. Yusuf felt so happy to be surrounded by his friends and family.

As the day came to an end, Yusuf and his family sat together, feeling thankful for the wonderful day they had. Yusuf's Baba explained, "Eid al-Fitr is important because it is a time to celebrate the end of Ramadan, a month of fasting and prayer. It is a time to thank Allah for His blessings and to share joy with family and friends."

"Eid is also a time to remember those who are less fortunate," Ummi added. "We give Zakat al-Fitr, a special charity, to help those in need."

Baba continued, "There is another important Eid called Eid al-Adha, which comes after the Hajj pilgrimage. Eid al-Adha commemorates the willingness of Prophet Ibrahim to sacrifice his son as an act of obedience to Allah. Allah provided a ram to sacrifice instead. On Eid al-Adha, we remember this act of faith and sacrifice animals, sharing the meat with family, friends, and the poor."

"Alhamdulillah for these beautiful Eid days," Yusuf said with a big smile.

Before going to bed, Yusuf whispered a prayer, "Thank you, Allah, for the joy of Eid and for my family and friends. Please bless us with many more happy days like this."

Yusuf felt peaceful and happy as he drifted off to sleep, dreaming of the wonderful day he had spent with his loved ones.

Moral of the Story: Eid is a time to celebrate with family and friends, to share joy and happiness, and to thank Allah for His blessings. It also reminds us to help those in need. Always remember to be grateful for the special moments with your loved ones.

Chapter 37

Allah's Wisdom in Speaking Kindly

Once upon a time, in a small village, there lived a little boy named Ahmed. Ahmed was a cheerful and kind-hearted boy who loved to play with his friends. He lived with his Ummi, Baba, and younger sister, Ukhti Mariam. Ahmed always tried to use kind words, just like his Ummi and Baba taught him.

One sunny morning, Ahmed and his friends, Bilal and Fatima, went to the park to play. As they were playing, Ahmed noticed a new boy sitting alone on a bench. The boy looked sad and lonely. Ahmed remembered what his Ummi had told him, "Always be kind and make others feel welcome."

"Assalamu Alaikum," Ahmed greeted the new boy with a smile. "My name is Ahmed. What's your name?"

"Wa Alaikum Assalam," the boy replied, looking up with a shy smile. "My name is Hamza. I just moved here."

"Nice to meet you, Hamza," Ahmed said kindly. "Do you want to play with us?"

Hamza's face lit up. "Yes, I'd love to!" he said.

Ahmed introduced Hamza to Bilal and Fatima, and they all played together. They ran around, laughed, and had so much fun. Hamza felt happy and welcomed, thanks to Ahmed's kind words.

Later that day, Ahmed went home. His Ummi was in the kitchen, preparing lunch. "Assalamu Alaikum, Ummi," Ahmed greeted her.

"Wa Alaikum Assalam, Ahmed," Ummi replied with a smile. "How was your time at the park?"

"It was great, Ummi," Ahmed said. "I made a new friend named Hamza. He just moved here and was feeling lonely, so I invited him to play with us."

"Alhamdulillah, Ahmed. You did a wonderful thing," Ummi said, hugging him. "Kind words can make a big difference in someone's day."

That evening, Ahmed was doing his homework when his younger sister, Ukhti Mariam, came into the room. She looked upset. "Ahmed, I can't find my favorite doll," she said with tears in her eyes.

Ahmed remembered his Ummi's words about kindness. "Don't worry, Mariam. I'll help you find it," he said gently.

They looked all around the house, and finally, they found the doll under the sofa. "Here it is!" Ahmed said, handing the doll to his sister.

"Thank you, Ahmed," Mariam said, hugging her doll tightly. "You're the best brother."

Ahmed felt happy knowing he had helped his sister feel better. He realized that kind words and actions could make people feel loved and cared for.

The next day at school, Ahmed saw his friend Bilal looking sad. "What's wrong, Bilal?" Ahmed asked.

"I didn't do well on my test," Bilal replied. "I feel really bad about it."

Ahmed put his arm around Bilal's shoulder. "It's okay, Bilal. Everyone makes mistakes. You can try again next time, and I'm sure you'll do better. You're very smart."

Bilal smiled. "Thanks, Ahmed. Your words make me feel better."

When Ahmed got home, he told his Baba about his day. "Baba, I learned that kind words can make people feel happy and loved," he said.

"That's right, Ahmed," Baba replied. "Allah loves those who are kind and use gentle words. Always remember to speak kindly to everyone."

That night, as Ahmed lay in bed, he whispered a prayer, "Thank you, Allah, for teaching me the power of kind words. Please help me to always be kind to others."

Moral of the Story: Kind words can make a big difference in someone's day. Always remember to speak kindly to everyone, and Allah will be pleased with you.

Chapter 38

Allah's Gift of Friendship

Once upon a time, in a small village, lived a boy named Amir. Amir was kind and loved helping others. He lived with his Ummi, Baba, and younger brother, Akhi Bilal, in a cozy house with a big garden full of beautiful flowers. Every day, Amir would play in the garden, but he felt lonely because he had no friends to play with.

One sunny morning, Amir's Ummi said, "Amir, let's go to the market today. We need to buy some vegetables and fruits." Amir was excited because he loved going to the market. He held his Ummi's hand, and they walked through the village, greeting their neighbors with "Assalamu Alaikum."

At the market, Amir saw many colorful stalls with all kinds of fruits, vegetables, and toys. While his Ummi was buying vegetables, Amir noticed a boy sitting alone near a fruit stall. The boy looked sad, so Amir walked up to him and said, "Assalamu Alaikum, my name is Amir. What's your name?"

The boy looked up and smiled. "Wa Alaikum Assalam, my name is Zain," he replied. "I just moved here with my family, and I don't know anyone yet."

Amir's heart felt warm. He knew what it was like to feel lonely. "Would you like to be my friend?" Amir asked.

Zain's eyes lit up with joy. "Yes, I would love to!" he said.

Amir introduced Zain to his Ummi, and they all walked home together. On the way, Amir and Zain talked about their favorite games and toys. They laughed and shared stories, feeling happy to have found each other.

From that day on, Amir and Zain played together every day. They played hide-and-seek in the garden, built sandcastles, and rode their bikes around the village. They became the best of friends. Amir's garden was no longer a lonely place; it was filled with laughter and fun.

One day, while they were playing, Amir's Ummi called them inside. "Boys, would you like to help me make cookies?" she asked.

"Yes, please!" they both shouted with excitement.

Amir's Ummi showed them how to mix the dough, roll it out, and cut it into shapes. They made star-shaped and heart-shaped cookies. The kitchen was filled with the sweet smell of baking cookies.

While they waited for the cookies to bake, Amir's Ummi said, "Do you know why you two became friends?"

Amir and Zain looked at each other and shrugged.

"It is because Allah brings people together," she said with a warm smile. "Allah knows when someone needs a friend and helps them find each other. Just like He brought you two together."

Amir and Zain smiled. They were thankful to Allah for their friendship.

As they enjoyed the delicious cookies, Amir's Ummi continued, "Always remember to be kind and open your heart to others. You never know when you might make a new friend."

Amir and Zain nodded. They promised to always be kind and to help others, just like Allah helped them find each other.

Amir and Zain's friendship grew stronger. They shared their toys, helped each other with homework, and always had fun together.

Moral of the Story: Allah brings people together to form friendships. Always be kind and open your heart to others. You never know when you might make a new friend.

Chapter 39

Allah's Colorful Masterpiece

Once upon a time, in a lovely little village, there was a young boy named Amin. Amin loved to explore the world around him. He was always curious and full of questions, especially about the colors of things he saw every day.

One bright morning, Amin's teacher, Ms. Fatima, decided to talk about a special gift that everyone in the class had—the gift of sight. "Today, we are going to learn about how we see and why being able to see is a blessing from Allah," she announced with a smile.

Amin was very excited and listened intently. Ms. Fatima explained, "Allah has given us eyes so we can see the beautiful world. Our eyes help us to learn, to read, and to see all the wonderful colors around us."

To show everyone just how special their sight was, Ms. Fatima planned a little adventure around the school. First, she took them to the school garden. "Look at all the flowers," she said. "Can you see how many different colors there are?"

Amin looked around and saw flowers in red, yellow, blue, and many more colors. He was amazed at how vibrant everything looked. "It's like a rainbow on the ground!" he exclaimed.

Next, they visited the art room where colorful paintings and drawings filled the walls. "Our ability to see lets us enjoy these beautiful artworks," Ms. Fatima explained. "Imagine if we couldn't see these colors, how different our experience would be."

Amin thought about it and felt thankful for his eyes.

Then, the class went to the playground. Ms. Fatima pointed to the sky and asked, "What do you see up there?"

The children looked up and saw the sky was a brilliant blue with fluffy white clouds drifting by. Amin felt so happy to see such a beautiful day.

Finally, they returned to their classroom where Ms. Fatima showed them a book with pictures of animals from all around the world. "Our eyes help us to learn about these creatures, their colors, and their homes. Without our sight, we wouldn't know what they look like," she said.

Amin was fascinated. He loved seeing the pictures of tigers, elephants, and colorful birds. It made him realize how much there was to see and learn.

After the adventure, Ms. Fatima sat down with all the children. "Did you all enjoy seeing all those wonderful things?" she asked.

"Yes!" all the children shouted happily.

Ms. Fatima smiled and said, "Being able to see is a precious gift from Allah. We should always be thankful for it because it allows us to see the beauty of the world He created for us."

Amin nodded and felt a deep sense of gratitude. He thought about how he used his eyes every day to learn and explore.

From that day on, Amin made sure to notice all the beautiful colors and sights around him. He knew that not everyone had the gift of sight, so he was extra thankful for his.

Later that evening, as Amin lay in bed, he whispered a prayer. "Thank you, Allah, for my eyes and the ability to see the beautiful world you created. Alhamdulillah."

Moral of the Story: Seeing is a wonderful gift from Allah. It allows us to enjoy the beauty of His creation. Always be thankful for your ability to see the world in its full glory.

Chapter 40

Allah's Blessing in Helping Hands

One morning, Yusuf's Ummi said, "Today is a special day at the community center. We are going to help pack food for people who need it. Would you like to come and help, Yusuf?"

Yusuf nodded eagerly. "Yes, Ummi! I would love to help!"

At the community center, Yusuf saw many tables filled with food like bread, fruits, and vegetables. His job was to put the food into boxes. Next to him, an older lady was trying to carry a heavy box, but it was too big for her.

"Can I help you with that?" Yusuf asked politely.

The lady smiled. "Oh, thank you, Yusuf! You are such a kind boy."

Yusuf felt happy inside as he helped the lady. He liked making others smile.

After the community center, Yusuf and his Ummi walked home. On the way, they saw an old man trying to cross the street. The man was moving very slowly because he was not very strong.

"Let's help him cross the street," Yusuf said to his Ummi.

Together, they walked over and asked, "Can we help you cross the street, sir?"

The old man was thankful. "Yes, please. Thank you, young man."

Yusuf held the man's hand and carefully helped him across the street. The man patted Yusuf's head and said, "Bless you, child. You have a good heart."

Feeling proud and happy, Yusuf continued walking home. He saw a cat stuck in a small tree. The cat was mewing softly, looking scared.

"I'll help you," Yusuf whispered to the cat. Carefully, he climbed up and gently picked up the cat, bringing it safely to the ground.

Just then, the cat's owner came running. "Oh, thank you! You saved my cat!" she exclaimed.

Yusuf just smiled and petted the cat. He felt wonderful helping others.

Feeling joyful and content, Yusuf discussed his feelings about the day with his Ummi as they walked home. "Ummi, I helped a lady, an old man, and even a cat today!" he shared excitedly.

His Ummi smiled warmly at him as they walked hand in hand. "I saw, Yusuf. You did so many good deeds today," she replied, squeezing his hand gently.

Yusuf beamed with pride. "It made me really happy to help them," he said.

"And it should," his Ummi nodded. "Helping others is not just about the actions we do; it's about the happiness and relief we bring to others. It's a beautiful way to show our love for Allah and to spread kindness in the world."

As they reached their home, Yusuf felt a deep sense of satisfaction. His Ummi's words made him realize that his actions were more than just helpful—they were meaningful. He made a silent promise to himself to continue doing good deeds, knowing each one made a difference.

That night, as Yusuf lay in bed, he couldn't help but smile as he thought about the gratitude and joy his actions had brought. He knew he would always look for ways to help people every day because he understood how much every act of kindness mattered.

Moral of the Story: Helping others is a beautiful way to show our love for Allah. Every act of kindness makes the world a better place.

Chapter 41

Allah's Amazing Human Body

In a small village, there lived a curious boy named Ali. Ali loved to ask questions about everything he saw. One sunny morning, Ali's ummi called him for breakfast. "Bismillah," Ali said before taking his first bite. His ummi smiled, happy to see him remember Allah.

After breakfast, Ali and his ummi went to visit his jaddi. When they arrived, Ali ran up to his jaddi and gave him a big hug. "Assalamu Alaikum, Jaddi!" he said.

"Wa Alaikum Assalam, Ali," his jaddi replied. "What are you curious about today?"

"Jaddi, can you tell me about the human body? How does it work?" Ali asked eagerly.

"Of course, Ali," his jaddi said. "Let's sit down, and I will tell you about the amazing body Allah has given us."

They sat under a big tree, and Jaddi began to explain. "Our body is like a machine that Allah created. It is made up of many parts, and each part has a special job."

"Like what, Jaddi?" Ali asked.

"Well," Jaddi said, "our heart is like a pump. It pumps blood all around our body. The blood carries oxygen and nutrients to all our parts. Every time it beats, it says 'Alhamdulillah' for the life Allah gives."

Ali put his hand on his chest and felt his heart beating. "That's amazing, Jaddi!"

"Our lungs help us breathe," Jaddi continued. "When we breathe in, we take in oxygen. When we breathe out, we get rid of what our body doesn't need."

Ali took a deep breath and let it out slowly. "Alhamdulillah for my lungs," he said.

Jaddi smiled. "Yes, Ali. And our brain is like a computer. It helps us think, learn, and remember. It also tells our body what to do."

"Our brain is so smart, Jaddi!" Ali said, tapping his head gently.

"Indeed," Jaddi agreed. "Our stomach helps us digest food. When we eat, our stomach breaks down the food so our body can use it for energy."

"Like when I eat my favorite dates, right?" Ali asked.

"Exactly," Jaddi said. "And our muscles help us move. We can run, jump, and play because of our muscles."

Ali stretched his arms and wiggled his fingers. "I'm so thankful for my muscles!"

"Our skin protects our body," Jaddi added. "It keeps out germs and helps us feel things like hot and cold."

Ali touched the grass and felt its coolness. "Alhamdulillah for my skin," he said.

"Every part of our body has a special job," Jaddi concluded. "Allah made us in the best way."

Ali looked up at his jaddi with wide eyes. "Allah's creation is wonderful, Jaddi. I'm so thankful for my body."

"Yes, Ali," Jaddi said, hugging him. "Always remember to take care of your body and thank Allah for His blessings."

That evening, as Ali got ready for bed, he thought about all the amazing things his body could do. He whispered, "Alhamdulillah for my heart, my lungs, my brain, and all my body parts."

Ali fell asleep with a smile on his face, grateful for the miracle of the human body.

Moral of the Story: Allah created our bodies with great wisdom and care. Every part of our body has a special job, and we should always be thankful to Allah for His amazing creation.

Chapter 42

Allah's Colorful Butterflies

In a lively village filled with flowers and trees, there was a small garden that was home to the most beautiful butterflies. In this garden lived a young girl named Ayesha, who loved to watch these colorful creatures flutter from flower to flower.

One sunny day, Ayesha's teacher, Miss Noor, took the whole class to the garden to learn about butterflies. "Assalamu Alaikum, children! Today, we are going to learn about Allah's beautiful creations: butterflies!" Miss Noor announced with a smile.

Ayesha was thrilled. She loved butterflies more than anything. They were like little flying jewels.

As they walked into the garden, Miss Noor started to explain, "Butterflies show us how creative Allah can be. Look at their wings! Each butterfly has its own pattern and colors."

Ayesha and her friends gathered around Miss Noor, who held a large, colorful book. She opened it to a page showing a picture of a butterfly. "This is a monarch butterfly," she explained. "See its orange wings with black and white spots? Each pattern is unique, made perfectly by Allah."

The children were amazed. They looked around and saw many butterflies around them, each different from the last.

"Now, let's play a little game," Miss Noor suggested. "I want each of you to find a butterfly and look closely at its wings. See if you can find one that looks exactly like another."

Excited, the children ran around the garden, peering at different butterflies. Ayesha found a butterfly with bright blue wings edged in black. She watched it dance in the air and land gently on a yellow flower.

"I found one, Miss Noor!" Ayesha called out, pointing to her butterfly.

Miss Noor came over and admired the butterfly with Ayesha. "That's a blue morpho, Ayesha. It's very special. Do you see how its wings shine in the sun?"

"Yes, it looks like it has lights on its wings," Ayesha replied, her eyes wide with wonder.

Miss Noor nodded. "Exactly! Allah has made each butterfly special. Just like He made each one of you special."

All the children gathered around again, each eager to share about the butterflies they had found. They talked about the colors and patterns, and no two butterflies were the same.

"Remember," Miss Noor said as they prepared to leave the garden, "just like these butterflies, each of you is unique and wonderfully made by Allah. We should always be thankful for the beautiful things He creates and take care of them."

Ayesha thought about the blue morpho as they walked back to school. She felt happy and special, knowing that Allah had created so many beautiful things in the world.

Each day after that, Ayesha would visit the garden, looking at the butterflies and remembering Miss Noor's words. She learned to see the beauty in every little thing and knew that everything around her was a sign of Allah's love.

Moral of the Story: Every butterfly is unique and beautiful in its own way, showing us how Allah is creative and loves beauty. We should appreciate and care for all of His creations.

Chapter 43

Allah's Garden of Fairness

Once upon a time, in a peaceful village, there was a lovely garden called "The Fair Garden." This garden was filled with the most beautiful flowers and plants. Every day, children from the village would come to play and enjoy the colorful blossoms.

In this village, there lived a kind-hearted boy named Ahmed. Ahmed loved spending time in The Fair Garden, and he often helped the gardener, Jaddi Ibrahim, take care of the plants. Ahmed enjoyed learning about the different flowers and how to make them grow strong and healthy.

One sunny morning, Jaddi Ibrahim called Ahmed over. "Assalamu Alaikum, Ahmed," he said with a warm smile.

"Wa Alaikum Assalam, Jaddi," Ahmed replied cheerfully.

"Today, I want to teach you something important," Jaddi Ibrahim said. "We must make sure every plant gets enough sunlight, water, and care. Allah has given us this beautiful garden, and it is our duty to take good care of it."

Ahmed nodded eagerly. "Bismillah, Jaddi! I am ready to learn."

As they walked through the garden, Jaddi Ibrahim showed Ahmed how to water the plants evenly and make sure each one had enough space to grow. Ahmed noticed a small flower that was hidden under a large bush.

"Jaddi, this flower isn't getting enough sunlight," Ahmed said.

"You are right, Ahmed. We must move it to a better spot," Jaddi Ibrahim replied. They carefully transplanted the flower to a sunnier location.

Later that day, Ahmed's friends, Amina and Bilal, came to play in the garden. Ahmed shared what he had learned with them. "We need to make sure every plant is treated fairly," he explained. "Just like Allah wants us to be kind and fair to everyone."

Amina and Bilal listened carefully. "That makes sense," Amina said. "We should treat everyone with kindness and fairness."

As they played, Ahmed saw a butterfly with a broken wing struggling to fly. "Oh no, this butterfly needs our help!" he exclaimed.

They gently picked up the butterfly and placed it on a flower where it could rest and find food. "Alhamdulillah, we were able to help," Bilal said with a smile.

The next day, Ahmed and his friends returned to The Fair Garden. They saw that the flower they had moved was standing tall and bright. The butterfly they had helped was now flying happily from flower to flower.

"See how everything flourishes when we care for it properly?" Jaddi Ibrahim said. "Allah has given us this garden to teach us the importance of fairness and kindness."

Ahmed felt proud of their efforts. "Thank you, Jaddi, for teaching us how to take care of the garden and each other."

"Alhamdulillah, Ahmed. Always remember to be fair and kind, just as Allah wants us to be," Jaddi Ibrahim said.

From that day on, Ahmed, Amina, and Bilal made sure to treat everyone and everything in the garden with fairness and kindness. They understood that just as the garden thrived under their care, so did their friendships and their community.

Moral of the Story: Fairness and kindness make the world a better place. Treat everyone and everything with care, just as Allah wants us to do.

Chapter 44

Allah's Busy Bees

In a small, cheerful village, there lived a young boy named Bilal. Bilal was curious and loved to learn about the world around him. He lived with his family in a cozy house with a beautiful garden full of colorful flowers.

One sunny morning, Bilal's Jaddi said, "Bilal, let's visit the farm today. I want to show you something special."

Bilal was excited. "Yes, Jaddi! I can't wait to see what it is!" he said, jumping with joy.

When they arrived at the farm, Bilal saw many different animals. There were cows, chickens, and even a horse. But what caught his attention the most was a big wooden box buzzing with activity.

"What's that, Jaddi?" Bilal asked, pointing to the box.

"That, Bilal, is a beehive," Jaddi explained. "Inside, there are many busy bees working hard to make honey. Let's go take a closer look."

As they walked closer, Bilal could hear the buzzing sound getting louder. He saw bees flying in and out of the hive. "Wow, there are so many bees!" Bilal exclaimed.

"Yes, Bilal," Jaddi said. "Allah has created bees to be very hardworking. Each bee has a special job to do. Some bees collect nectar from flowers, while others stay in the hive to make honey."

Bilal watched in amazement as the bees buzzed around the flowers, collecting nectar. "Why do bees make honey, Jaddi?" he asked.

"Honey is their food," Jaddi explained. "But Allah has also made honey special for us. It's sweet and good for our health. Bees work together to make honey, and it teaches us the importance of teamwork and hard work."

Bilal thought about this and felt grateful. "Alhamdulillah, Allah has made bees so amazing," he said.

Jaddi smiled. "Yes, Bilal. And we should always remember to thank Allah for His creations."

When they returned home, Bilal couldn't stop thinking about the bees. He wanted to share what he had learned with his family. "Ummi, Baba, guess what I saw today?" Bilal said excitedly.

"What did you see, Bilal?" Ummi asked, smiling at her son's enthusiasm.

"I saw bees making honey! They work so hard and have special jobs. And Jaddi told me that honey is good for us," Bilal explained.

"That's wonderful, Bilal," Baba said. "It's important to appreciate Allah's creations and learn from them."

As Bilal went to bed that night, he thought about the busy bees and how hard they worked. He felt inspired to work hard and be helpful, just like the bees. He whispered a prayer, "Thank you, Allah, for the bees and their honey. Please help me to always be hardworking and thankful."

From that day on, Bilal always remembered the lesson he learned from the bees. He worked hard in school, helped his family at home, and was kind to his friends. He knew that being busy and helpful, like the bees, was a good way to show his love for Allah and His creations.

Moral of the Story: Just like the busy bees, we should work hard and help each other. Always be thankful for Allah's creations and the lessons they teach us.

Chapter 45

Allah's Blessing of Taste

In a colorful town, there was a cheerful boy named Sami. Sami loved eating different kinds of food. His favorite time was mealtime because he enjoyed tasting all sorts of flavors.

One day, Sami's school decided to have a "Taste Day." The teacher, Mrs. Fatima, told the class, "Today, we will explore the gift of taste that Allah has given us. We will try different foods and talk about how they taste."

Sami was very excited. He loved trying new things!

Mrs. Fatima brought in several foods for the children to try: lemons, honey, nuts, and dates. She lined up the foods on a big table, and all the children gathered around.

"First, we have lemons," said Mrs. Fatima. She gave a small piece to each child. When Sami tasted his lemon, he made a funny face because it was sour. "Lemons are sour," Sami said, giggling.

Next, they tried the honey. It was smooth and sweet. Sami loved it! "Honey is sweet," he said with a smile.

Then, they tasted the nuts. "Nuts are a bit crunchy and salty," Sami noticed. He liked how the saltiness mixed with the crunch.

Last, they tried the dates. Dates were sweet and chewy. Sami thought they were delicious. "Dates are sweet like honey, but they feel different in my mouth," he explained.

After tasting all the foods, Mrs. Fatima said, "Allah has given us our taste buds so we can enjoy different flavors. Whether it's sour, sweet, salty, or bitter, every taste is special."

Sami thought about what Mrs. Fatima said. He realized how wonderful it was to taste different things. "It's like a gift because not everyone in the world can taste like we do," he whispered to his friend.

Mrs. Fatima heard him and nodded. "Yes, Sami. Being able to taste is a special gift from Allah. We should be thankful for it and also remember to eat foods that are good for us."

The children spent the rest of the day talking about their favorite foods and the different tastes they loved. Sami enjoyed learning about the tastes and was grateful for the gift of taste.

Every mealtime at home, Sami would now think about how each food tasted. He would say, "Thank you, Allah, for this tasty food," before he ate.

Sami started to appreciate his meals more and even tried to guess what ingredients were in his food just by tasting it. His yumma was happy to see him enjoying his food and learning about the flavors.

As Sami grew older, he always remembered the "Taste Day" at school. It taught him not just about the flavors but also to be thankful for the little things in life, like the ability to taste.

Moral of the Story: The ability to taste is a wonderful gift from Allah. We should appreciate it and enjoy the variety of flavors He has created for us.

Chapter 46

Allah's Art in Snowflakes

In the small, quiet town of Hajar, winter was everyone's favorite season, especially for little Amina. She loved watching the snowfall, each flake dancing like a tiny star down to earth.

One chilly morning, Amina's teacher, Mr. Jamal, announced, "Assalamu Alaikum, today we're going to learn about snowflakes, Allah's special winter art!"

Amina was excited. She loved snow but had never thought about it like that before.

Mr. Jamal started the class with a smile, "Did you know that every snowflake is different? Each one has its own shape, no two are ever the same. This is a sign of Allah's creativity."

He held up a large, clear picture of a snowflake. "Look closely," he said. "See all the patterns? It's like a beautiful flower made of ice."

The children crowded around to see. Each pattern was detailed and delicate, like a tiny masterpiece.

"Wow," Amina whispered. She wondered how something so small could have such detailed designs.

Mr. Jamal continued, "Just like snowflakes, each of you is unique. Allah made every one of you special in your own way."

He then gave each child a magnifying glass. "We're going to catch our own snowflakes today and look at them before they melt. Let's see how many patterns we can find!"

The children bundled up in their warmest coats and rushed outside, their magnifying glasses ready. It was snowing gently, perfect for catching snowflakes.

Amina held out her black mitten, watching eagerly as snowflakes landed on it. Through her magnifying glass, she saw the intricate details of each snowflake. Some looked like stars, others like tiny webs.

"Each one is a little different!" she exclaimed, fascinated by their designs.

Her friends called out excitedly about their snowflakes too. "This one looks like a feather!" "Mine is like a spiderweb!"

Back in the classroom, Mr. Jamal asked, "What did you all notice about your snowflakes?"

"They're all different," said Amina, "and so pretty."

"Yes," Mr. Jamal nodded. "Allah's creativity is limitless. He creates these tiny wonders, each a work of art. Just like each of you, every snowflake plays its part in making winter so beautiful."

The children spent the afternoon drawing pictures of the snowflake patterns they had seen. Amina drew hers with careful, curving lines.

"Today, I learned that snowflakes are special, just like us," Amina said as she added the last touch to her drawing.

Mr. Jamal smiled. "Exactly, Amina. And every time it snows, remember that each snowflake is a reminder of how unique and creative Allah is."

From that day, every snowfall made Amina think of Allah's creativity. She loved catching snowflakes and remembering that, like the snowflakes, she was special in her own way.

Moral of the Story: Every snowflake is unique and beautiful, just like each of us. Allah's creativity is in everything around us, reminding us to appreciate the uniqueness in ourselves and in the world.

Chapter 47

Allah's Wisdom in the Sense of Touch

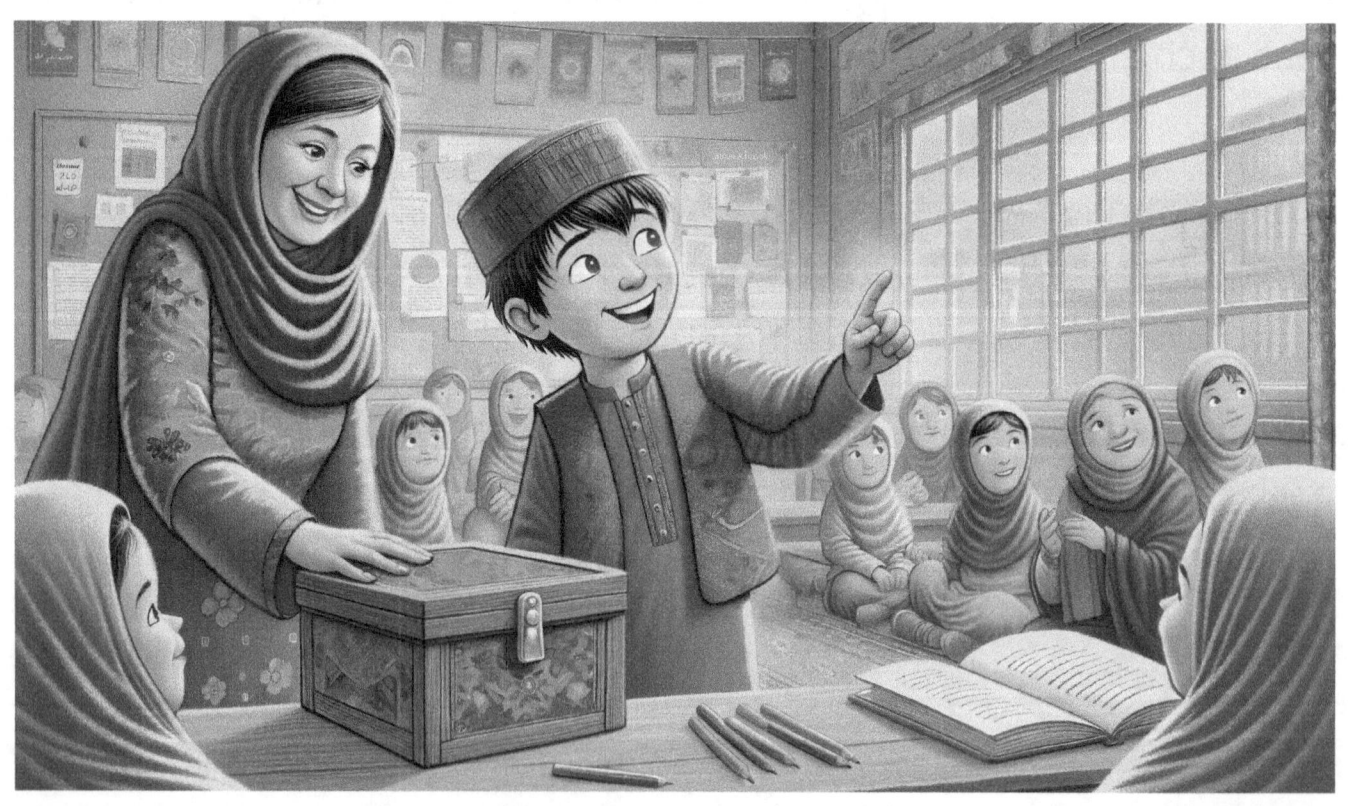

In the small village of Noor, there was a kind-hearted boy named Youssef. Youssef loved exploring the world around him, especially through touch. He loved to feel the rough bark of trees, the soft fur of his cat, and the cool water of the river.

One sunny day, Youssef's teacher, Miss Sara, planned a special lesson about the senses. "Assalamu Alaikum, today, we're going to learn about a wonderful gift from Allah—the gift of touch," she announced to the class.

Youssef was excited. He already loved feeling different textures.

Miss Sara brought out a mystery box filled with objects. "You'll each get a chance to feel something from the box without looking. Then, you can guess what it is!" she explained.

When it was Youssef's turn, he reached into the box and felt something smooth and round. After thinking for a moment, he guessed, "It's a marble!"

"That's right, Youssef!" Miss Sara said with a smile. "Can you tell us how it felt?"

"It was smooth and a little cold," Youssef described.

Miss Sara nodded. "Our sense of touch helps us learn about the world. It tells us if something is hot or cold, smooth or rough, and so much more."

The class continued, and Youssef felt more objects—a soft scarf, a prickly pinecone, and a squishy sponge. Each texture was a new discovery.

After the activity, Miss Sara gathered everyone for a story. "Allah has given us the ability to touch and feel so we can better understand and appreciate the world He created for us," she began.

"Imagine if we couldn't feel," she continued. "We wouldn't know the warmth of a hug from our family or the cool breeze on a hot day. Our sense of touch is a blessing that helps us connect with others and our surroundings."

Youssef listened intently. He had never thought about how important touch was before.

"For homework," Miss Sara added, "I want you to find three things at home that feel different and bring them to class tomorrow. We'll share how each one feels."

Youssef was excited for the assignment. That evening, he explored his house and chose three things: his fluffy pillow, a smooth pebble from the garden, and his sticky honey jar.

The next day, Youssef shared his items with the class. "This pillow feels soft and makes me feel sleepy," he laughed. "The pebble is hard and cool, and the honey jar is sticky, but it smells sweet!"

Miss Sara praised him, "Very good, Youssef! You're becoming very thoughtful about the world around you."

From that day on, Youssef paid more attention to how things felt. He appreciated the softness of his yumma's hand and the roughness of the sand under his feet.

He realized that every sensation was a gift from Allah, meant to be cherished and appreciated.

Moral of the Story: The ability to touch and feel is a special gift from Allah. It helps us learn about our world and appreciate the many textures and sensations. Always remember to be thankful for this wonderful sense.

Chapter 48

Allah's Bounty in Paradise

In a small, sunny village, there lived a little girl named Laila. Laila loved listening to stories, especially the ones her jaddati told about Paradise. One of her favorite stories was about the wonderful fruits that grow there.

One peaceful evening, Laila and her jaddati were sitting in their garden. Laila was enjoying a juicy orange and looked up at her jaddati with curious eyes. "Jadda, is it true that in Paradise, there are fruits even more delicious than these?" she asked.

Her jaddati smiled and nodded. "Yes, my dear. In Paradise, Allah has fruits that we can't even imagine. They are sweeter than any fruit we have here, and they never run out."

Laila's eyes widened with wonder. "What kind of fruits are there in Paradise?" she asked eagerly.

"Well," her jaddati began, "there are fruits like apples and oranges, but much, much tastier. There are also fruits that we've never seen before, each one unique and bursting with flavor."

Laila thought about this and then asked, "Do they look different too?"

"Yes, they are bright and colorful, with wonderful smells that fill the air," her jaddati explained. "Each fruit is perfect and refreshing."

Laila imagined a place filled with colorful, delicious fruits of all shapes and sizes. She could almost taste them just by thinking about it.

"Jadda, why does Allah give us such special fruits in Paradise?" Laila wondered aloud.

Her jaddati took her hand gently. "Allah wants to reward us for our good deeds. When we are kind, help others, and remember Allah, we are promised the beautiful gifts of Paradise."

Laila looked around at the garden and then back at her orange. "So, every good thing I do here can help me taste the fruits in Paradise?" she asked.

"Yes, exactly!" her jaddati replied with a proud smile. "Every good deed is like planting a seed. If we take care of it by doing more good deeds, it grows, and Allah rewards us with the fruits of Paradise."

Laila felt happy thinking about doing good deeds. She wanted to be sure she could one day taste the special fruits her jaddati described.

"Let's promise to always do our best to be kind and do good things," Laila said with determination.

Her jaddati hugged her. "That's a wonderful promise. And remember, Laila, Allah's gifts are not just fruits but also happiness and peace for always being kind and good."

Every day after that, Laila tried her best to be helpful and kind. She knew that even the smallest good deed was important. She looked forward to the day she could enjoy the amazing fruits of Paradise that Allah had promised.

As the stars began to twinkle in the evening sky, Laila felt grateful for her jaddati's stories that taught her about the beautiful rewards awaiting in Paradise.

Moral of the Story: Allah has prepared wonderful rewards like the fruits of Paradise for those who do good deeds. Always remember to be kind and do good, and one day, you may enjoy the sweetest fruits you can ever imagine.

Chapter 49

Allah's Guidance in Honesty

In a friendly village lived a little boy named Ahmed. Ahmed was known for his bright smile and cheerful attitude. He loved playing with his friends and listening to stories from his parents. One day, Ahmed's baba told him a story about honesty. "Ahmed," he began, "being honest is very important. It pleases Allah and helps us become better people."

Ahmed listened carefully, wanting to learn more.

The next day at school, Ahmed's teacher, Miss Amina, made an exciting announcement. "Assalamu Alaikum, we are going to have a drawing contest! The winner will get a special prize." Ahmed loved drawing and was excited to join. He spent the entire afternoon planning what he would draw. He wanted his picture to be the best.

When he got home, Ahmed started working on his drawing. He decided to draw a beautiful picture of a tree with birds and flowers. He worked very hard, coloring each part carefully and adding lots of details. By the end, he was very proud of his work.

The next morning, on his way to school, Ahmed saw a beautiful drawing on the ground. It was even better than his! The drawing showed a colorful garden with butterflies and flowers, and it looked amazing. He picked it up and thought, "If I use this drawing, I might win the contest."

Ahmed stood there for a moment, holding the drawing. But then he remembered his baba's story about honesty. He knew that taking someone else's drawing and saying it was his own would not be honest. It would be cheating, and it would not please Allah.

At school, all the children showed their drawings to Miss Amina. Ahmed showed his own drawing, not the one he found. He felt a little nervous because he really wanted to win, but he knew he was doing the right thing.

Later that day, Miss Amina announced the winner. It was not Ahmed. He felt a little sad because he had worked so hard, but he also felt proud because he had been honest.

After school, Ahmed's friend Ali came running to him. "Ahmed, I lost my drawing! I think I dropped it on the way to school," he said, looking very upset.

Ahmed realized that the beautiful drawing he found was Ali's. "Ali, I found your drawing," Ahmed said. He took it out of his bag and gave it to Ali.

"Jazak Allah Khair, Ahmed!" Ali said with a big smile. "I was so worried I lost it forever."

Ahmed felt happy. He knew he had done the right thing by being honest. When he got home, he told his baba what had happened. His baba hugged him and said, "I am very proud of you, Ahmed. You showed honesty, and that pleases Allah. You did a good deed today."

That night, Ahmed thought about how good it felt to be honest. He knew that even though he didn't win the contest, he had done something much more important. He had made his friend happy and pleased Allah.

From that day on, Ahmed always tried to be honest in everything he did. He knew that honesty was a special quality that made him a better person. He also learned that doing the right thing feels good, even if no one else knows.

Moral of the Story: Being honest pleases Allah and makes us better people. Always tell the truth and do the right thing, even if it's hard.

Chapter 50

Allah's Knowledge in the Natural World

In a peaceful village nestled between mountains and rivers, there lived a curious boy named Sami. Sami loved to explore nature and discover its many wonders. One day, his baba decided to take him on a walk through the forest to teach him about Allah's wisdom in nature.

As they walked, Sami noticed a tall tree with deep roots and wide branches. He was fascinated by its size and strength. "Baba, why do trees have such big roots?" Sami asked, his eyes wide with curiosity.

His baba smiled and said, "Allah, in His wisdom, made trees with strong roots to hold them firmly in the ground. The roots help the tree stand tall and get water and nutrients from the soil. Just like we need food and water to grow, trees do too."

Sami thought about how smart that was. He noticed how the tree provided shade and a home for birds and insects. He saw birds building nests and ants crawling up the bark. "Allah made trees so useful," he said, feeling a deep sense of wonder.

"Yes, Sami," his baba replied. "Trees give us shade, fruit, and oxygen to breathe. They are one of Allah's many blessings. We should always appreciate and take care of them."

As they walked further, they reached a flowing river. Sami watched the water rushing over the rocks and saw fish swimming and plants growing near the water. "Baba, why is the river important?" he asked, dipping his fingers into the cool water.

"The river is important because it brings water to all the plants and animals that live near it," his baba explained. "Allah made rivers to flow through the land, providing life and nourishment to everything around them."

Sami watched the water sparkle in the sunlight and thought about how it helped so many living things. He saw frogs hopping along the banks and birds drinking from the river. "Allah's wisdom is amazing," he said, feeling awe-struck.

They continued their walk and came across a beehive. Sami watched the bees buzzing around, busy collecting nectar from flowers. "Baba, why do bees work so hard?" Sami wondered, watching a bee land on a flower.

"Allah gave bees the wisdom to make honey," his baba said. "Bees collect nectar from flowers and turn it into honey, which is sweet and delicious. Honey is also good for our health. The bees work together in a hive, each one knowing its role, just as Allah planned."

Sami marveled at how everything in nature had a purpose and worked together. He saw the bees flying back to their hive, carrying nectar. "Allah is very wise," he said, feeling grateful for the bees and their hard work.

"Yes, Sami. Allah's wisdom is everywhere in nature. From the smallest insect to the largest tree, everything has a place and a purpose," his baba agreed.

As they walked back home, Sami thought about all the things he had learned. He felt grateful for Allah's wisdom in creating such a beautiful and balanced world. He realized how everything in nature was connected and how each part played an important role.

Moral of the Story: Allah's wisdom is shown in every part of nature. From trees and rivers to bees and stars, everything has a purpose and place. Always appreciate and be thankful for the wonders of the natural world.

www.ingramcontent.com/pod-product-compliance
Lightning Source LLC
Chambersburg PA
CBHW082337300426
44109CB00045B/2401